PROGRAM EVALUATION
IN MORAL EDUCATION

Hugh F. Cline
Robert A. Feldmesser

Educational Testing Service
Princeton, New Jersey 08541

Table of Contents

Acknowledgments

It is impossible to express adequately our appreciation to all those who so graciously provided assistance in the preparation of this handbook. However, we wish especially to acknowledge both the financial support of the Danforth Foundation and the intellectual support of Gene Schwilck and Geraldine Bagby, its President and Vice President, respectively. Furthermore, we express our appreciation for the substantive guidance of Robert J. Solomon, Executive Vice President of Educational Testing Service, as well as the contributions of our research colleagues, Marianne Amarel, Jerilee E. Grandy, Frieda M. Hardy, Loraine T. Sinnott, and Gita Z. Wilder.

The following people provided indispensable assistance to us in carrying out the fieldwork: Todd Clark, Diane Farwick, Edwin Fenton, Gary Fornander, Diane Hedin, Maria Maracic, Nancy Mathews, Byron Schneider, and Stanley Toll.

A first draft of this report was read by William J. Bennett, R. Freeman Butts, Edwin Fenton, William J. Gephart, Howard Kirschenbaum, Maria Maracic, and Howard Mehlinger. Each of them gave us comments and raised questions that greatly improved the final product, but of course they are not responsible for any shortcomings that remain.

The cooperation and competence of Christine Sansone and her text processing staff expedited the work and made it more pleasant as well. Finally, without the administrative, editorial, and secretarial management of Lois G. Harris, this handbook could not have been completed. Her untimely death, not long after the final version had been printed, saddened us all. She will be remembered as a dedicated colleague and a friend.

Chapter One

INTRODUCTION

This handbook has been prepared to address one specific problem: How can the techniques of program evaluation be effectively applied to produce useful in formation about the operations and impact of moral education programs in secondary schools? The intended audiences are secondary-school personnel, school-board members, program sponsors, parents, and interested citizens. These two brief statements of the problem and the audience belie the vast complexity involved in the transfer of evaluation techniques used in other educational or social programs to the assessment of moral education in secondary schools.

During the past two decades, a variety of research and development activities have been undertaken in the closely related areas of moral, civic, ethics, and values education at the secondary-school level. Inevitably, questions arise about the effectiveness of these activities, questions that will be asked by their sponsors, originators, and users, and by educational practitioners who may be interested in initiating such programs in their school districts. Evaluation in the area of moral education encounters certain special difficulties, which are discussed at length in this volume. A careful study of the procedures employed in such programs has been undertaken both to learn how to cope with these difficulties and to build upon prior experience so that program developers, administrators, teachers, and others will have more effective tools with which to evaluate their efforts. This handbook is intended to be a manual of techniques for such program evaluation. Furthermore, it

1

is intended specifically to provide guidelines for adopting flexible, effective methods of data collection and analysis which will provide more systematic insights into the impact of their moral education programs.

The handbook is addressed to a number of groups. First are those secondary-school practitioners who are already engaged in moral education programs but who have not been satisfied with any evaluative efforts made thus far. The second audience consists of decision makers and practitioners who are considering the introduction of a moral education program in their schools. It seems very likely that a major deterrent to the introduction of a moral education program is uncertainty about the effects the program may produce, about how effects can be observed while the program is in progress and at some future point, and about how the results of the observations can be interpreted to promote rational discussion of next steps. This handbook is designed to provide guidance on all of these matters. Thus, we anticipate that the handbook may facilitate the adoption of moral education programs and permit the accumulation of valid and reliable information about their effects, to the advantage of future decision makers.

A third audience consists of the sponsors and developers of moral education programs whose interests lie in collecting evaluative information in order to improve their programs, to decide whether to continue with them and in what directions, and to be able to inform potential users about their effects. In addition to these three groups there are, of course, interested citizens and the general public, whose children are being exposed to these programs and who, therefore, have a right to the best possible understanding of their effects.

It is neither necessary nor desirable for this handbook to be an exhaustive treatise on the subject of educational evaluation. A lengthy or highly technical manual would not be widely used. What is intended, rather, is that the handbook present a concise discussion of what is involved in each step of an evaluation, give reference to other sources of additional information; and then concentrate on the special problems that arise in the context of moral education programs, on the methods that have been used or that can be suggested for dealing with these problems, and on the advantages and disadvantages for each of these methods.

On the other hand, readers will not find in this volume a ready-made approach to producing definitive evidence to support the continuation or expansion of moral education programs. However, those who are willing to make the effort to extract from this handbook procedures for evaluation and assessment which will provide a richer insight into the effects of such programs on students, teachers, schools, and communities will find an array of provocative discussions to enable them to tailor data collection and analysis techniques to meet the particular exigencies of their programs.

The handbook is divided into five chapters. The rest of this chapter is devoted to a brief description of the background and methods of the project which led to this handbook, a discussion of the major forms and functions of evaluation, and a review of the multiple, overlapping, and sometimes conflicting purposes of program evaluations. Chapter 2 discusses the nature of moral education and presents various types of programs within a four-category typology. This discussion both sets the boundaries for the scope of the handbook and provides an internal map for distinguishing among the various moral education programs.

Chapter 3 offers guidelines for designing evaluations of moral education programs. It discusses the importance of exploratory studies and the nature of causal analysis, and it reviews various experimental and quasi-experimental designs for moral education program evaluation. Chapter 4 then takes up the complex issues of specifying goals for moral education programs and identifying indicators of goal attainment. Chapter 5 addresses questions of data analysis. After briefly reviewing the issues of reliability and validity, the chapter comments on several problems in the analysis and reporting of the results of an evaluation to various audiences. The chapter includes a set of cautionary notes about some common pitfalls in program evaluation.

Following a "Postscript" which comments on the question of whether a school should introduce a moral education program, the volume concludes with several appendices. Appendix A includes brief descriptions of four prototypes of moral education programs. These prototypes are based upon the data collected during the course of preparing this handbook. They further illustrate the typology presented in Chapter 1. However, they are prototypes and do not correspond to any specific moral education program included in this study. Appendix B contains a bibliography of relevant literature concerning both moral education and evaluation. Appendix C contains the names, addresses, and brief annotations of additional sources of information concerning the development and evaluation of moral education programs.

Project methods

The origin of this handbook lies in a request made by the Danforth Foundation to Educational Testing Service to provide assistance in the evaluation of moral education programs. For many years, the Danforth Foundation has provided support to both social scientists and practicing educators to design, develop, field test, and disseminate a number of different moral education programs. As a logical corollary, it asked Educational Testing Service to undertake a project to determine what perspectives, research methodologies, and specific evaluation techniques might be useful in the general area of moral education, particularly as it is practiced in secondary schools. This volume, then, written by the co-directors of that project, is an attempt to take what is relevant from the burgeoning practice and literature of social-program evaluation and apply it to the specific problems of evaluating moral education programs.

In preparation for writing this handbook, we immersed ourselves in both the literature and practice of moral education programs. To accomplish this, three activities were completed: (a) a literature review; (b) visits to the leading centers of research and development in moral education; and (c) case studies of selected moral education programs in secondary schools. The literature on both moral education and evaluation was reviewed to determine the degree of fit between these fields, a connection which had not previously been systematically explored. The purpose of visits to research and development centers was to learn more about the history of specific programs and the views and experiences of some of the key figures in the field of moral education. Visits were made to Harvard University, Carnegie-Mellon University, Indiana University, the Ontario Institute for Studies in Education, the National Humanistic Education Center, the Constitutional Rights Foundation, and the Institute for Political and Legal Education.

The third set of activities preparatory to writing the handbook was a series of case studies of moral education programs. The primary aim of the case studies was to learn about evaluation procedures. The case studies also allowed a detailed analysis of the operation of the programs, an analysis essential to understanding how evaluation procedures could be improved and generalized to other settings. In order to test the data collection and analysis procedures for the case studies, pilot studies were undertaken in Indianapolis, Los Angeles, Pittsburgh, and Westport, Connecticut. After review of the pilot studies and appropriate refinements in the procedures, six case studies were made — of moral education programs in Bakersfield, California; Chicago; Colorado Springs, Colorado; Minneapolis; Ossining, New York; and Salt Lake City. Each of the pilot and case studies was completed by one of the authors and one other member of the ETS research staff. Site-visit activities included:

1. interviews with students, teachers, guidance counselors, administrators, and, where appropriate, representatives of various community agencies;
2. observation of class sessions and other program activities; and
3. observations of comparable classes not included in the program.

Field notes were recorded during all interviews and observations, and on the basis of these notes a formal report of each site visit was prepared and shared among the project staff. Each case-study report was also reviewed by those individuals with major operating responsibility for the program. Prototypes of the case studies appear in Appendix A to give the reader an understanding of the kinds of programs included in the project, as well as a sense of how a moral education program might look and operate in a real-life setting.

4

Types of evaluation

In recent decades evaluation research has become widely accepted and practiced as a unique and potentially important dimension in the planning and conduct of educational programs. A number of concurrent and related factors account for the increasing attention devoted to evaluation. First, due to declining resources available from both public and private sources to support education, there is a growing demand for accountability in all educational institutions. As the public has become increasingly concerned over the many widely publicized reports of declines in the educational performance of students, greater efforts have been made to determine why education has become less effective. In addition, pressures have mounted to determine the effects of specific educational programs and innovations.

Second, there is an increasing demand for precision and expertise in the design and implementation of educational programs. Positive intentions and dedicated work are no longer adequate to insure continued support of programs. Both educational administrators and the general public are aware of the disappointing results of many highly publicized and attractive innovations, and this has further contributed to the demand for more vigorous program review. Third, measurement technology has advanced significantly, and we now have the capacity for producing more comprehensive quantitative descriptions and analyses of educational programs and outcomes. The development and widespread distribution of more sophisticated educational measurement methods has made it possible for a large number of practitioners and researchers to undertake evaluation research efforts.

Despite the recent surge of activity in social experimentation and evaluation, the roots of these efforts can be traced back at least to the late nineteenth century when standardized spelling tests were used to determine if the length of time spent on drills improved performance. Subsequently, evaluations have been completed on a wide variety of topics, including the effects of health-education programs on individual hygienic practices, the effects of treatment programs on juvenile delinquents, and the effects of participation in an experimental college program on the political attitudes of students. With support from a number of public and private agencies, evaluation research became a major field of activity for many educational researchers. The Elementary and Secondary Education Act of 1965 formalized evaluation as a fundamental and pervasive activity in education, for it mandated evaluation of every funded program.

In recent years major evaluations have been completed of a wide variety of educational programs, including compensatory preschool programs, performance contract projects, and children's television programming. In each of these instances it was anticipated that the results of the evaluation research would provide specific recommendations pertinent to the initiation, continuation, expansion, modification, or elimination of programs. Although these initial expectations have largely been frustrated, each of these evaluation efforts produced a much greater appreciation of the complexities involved in designing and administering educational programs.

A careful reading of the literature of educational as well as other social-program evaluation reveals a consensus on two essential points, a consensus shared among all the leading figures in the field (Scriven, 1961; Stake, 1967; Suchman, 1967; Stufflebeam, 1971; Weiss, 1972; Riecken and Boruch, 1974; Caro, 1977; Guba, 1978; Rossi, Freeman, and Wright, 1979; Cronbach, 1980). The first is that verifiable and replicable procedures should be employed to collect information. The second is that judgment must be exercised in relating the information to program outcomes. Program evaluations indicate the extent to which these or other outcomes have been achieved. However, on only these two points is there consensus among the designers, promoters, practitioners, and critics of evaluation research. The remainder of the chapter will document the diversity among them.

For the purposes of our review in this handbook, we find it convenient to distinguish among four different forms of evaluation research: policy analysis, experimental designs, qualitative analysis, and eclectic designs. This classification is proposed for heuristic purposes. We do not claim that it is definitive or exhaustive or that the categories in the classification are mutually exclusive. The explication of these four types corresponds roughly to a chronological account of the development of evaluation research over the past several decades.

Since World War II, expenditures by government agencies, particularly at the federal level, for social and educational programs have increased dramatically, rapidly giving rise to the need for more information concerning the efficacy of these expenditures. It was in this milieu that policy analysis was born as a new field of applied social-science research. Initially concern was focused on calculating the costs incurred for the benefits obtained from alternative program expenditures. However, very soon a plethora of broader policy analysis perspectives arose, including the program-planning and budgeting procedures developed during the Kennedy administration. However, the narrow fiscal perspective of most policy analyses at that time were severely criticized, the critics pointing out that program costs and particularly benefits could rarely be quantified accurately in monetary terms. It was argued that the most important effects of most social and educational programs could not be reduced to such a one-dimensional metric.

These quite valid criticisms prompted a number of efforts to adapt the methods of the classic laboratory experiment to a field setting. Experimental design thus became the second major form of evaluation research. Promoted by many social scientists, this design attempted to adopt the characteristics of the true laboratory experiment, including randomized assignment, premeasurement, and postmeasurement. The intention here was to develop research designs and measurement instruments that would focus more directly on program goals. The experimental evaluation research design also gave rise to the requirement that program goals be specified in a fashion that allowed more precise measurement.

At this time evaluation research became a rapidly growing business activity. It involved many academic-based researchers and spawned a large number of both profit and not-for-profit research institutes devoted to evaluation research. Again, the expectation was that the experimental research would provide definitive answers with respect to policy decisions. Evaluation research was undertaken on many large-scale programs. However, these activities were followed by a period of intense disenchantment. It became clear that, in too many instances, inappropriate methods were used, some design features could not be maintained, and the results of the research played a negligible role in policy formation.

The criticisms of and frustration with experimental-design evaluation research gave rise to an attempt to provide much richer and more detailed qualitative analyses to complement or, in some instances, replace the outcome-orientation of the experimental design. The charge was made by many critics that the experimental design ignored many important features or activities associated with a program. The narrow focus on program goals and outcomes simply missed too many important characteristics of a program and produced rather sterile evaluation reports. These concerns promoted a variety of different types of qualitative evaluation research efforts.

At this point Michael Scriven further promoted the case for a qualitative perspective with his distinction between "formative" and "summative" evaluations (Scriven, 1967). Formative evaluation was that undertaken to produce information that provides immediate feedback for improvement in an ongoing program. In a formative evaluation the researcher examines program operations from many different perspectives. A formative evaluation tends to use more qualitative data collection and analysis procedures. Summative evaluation, on the other hand, was that designed to assess the outcomes of a program, and it tends to employ more quantitative analyses. More recently these terms have taken on additional connotations relating to both design features and data-analysis techniques. Because very few researchers are competent in the use of both qualitative and quantitative research methodologies, they tend to identify with one or the other of these perspectives. For the most part, there tends to be a mutually exclusive division of labor in educational evaluation research.

An incorrect assumption is frequently made that qualitative research can be completed more rapidly and is therefore appropriate to formative evaluation, which presupposes rapid feedback of results for immediate program implementation. However, carefully done qualitative research designs employing in-depth interviews and extensive participant observations frequently require more time than the quasi-experimental measurement research designs.

There are a number of different forms of qualitative evaluation. Stake (1967) has advocated one that focuses upon a program's antecedents, transactions, and outcomes, each of them to be analyzed in terms of intentions, observations, standards, and judgments. This approach to evaluation thus generates a three-by-four matrix that is useful for decisions concerning the future of a program. Stufflebeam (1971) proposed an approach to formative evaluation providing for program goals, inputs, operational decisions, and feedback. A discrepancy model that focuses on the difference between standards and performance has been offered by Provus (1971). Alkin (1969) and his colleagues at UCLA introduced a perspective with five major components: needs assessment, program planning, implementation evaluation, progress evaluation, and outcome evaluation.

Each of these perspectives emphasized the collection of qualitative data, which are then analyzed and summarized by the evaluator to produce information useful for decision making. The focus is on decisions made during the operation of a program, decisions that can adjust and fine-tune a program.

The fourth and most recent form of evaluation research, the eclectic design, was proposed by Cronbach and his associates at Stanford University (Cronbach, 1980). Cronbach feels strongly that prior perspectives on evaluation have been too narrowly focused. He argues for a more comprehensive approach that draws upon elements of cost-benefit analysis, experimental design, and qualitative evaluations as appropriate to meet the needs of specific programs and decision makers. Cronbach argues persuasively that evaluation research should not be undertaken with a rigid adherence to any one perspective. Alternatively, he suggests a strategy which is both more realistic and flexible in terms of accomplishments, outcomes, and the time and resources necessary to achieve effective evaluation.

Given this multiplicity of evaluation forms, one might ask how it is possible to determine which approach is most useful for the evaluation of a moral education program. In our view, the most promising approach is the eclectic design of Cronbach. In the remainder of this handbook we adopt this strategy and offer the reader specific guidelines and suggestions for how it may be applied to different types of moral education programs.

Today evaluation is widely accepted as an integral part of effective management, including planning, development, implementation, and evaluation. However, within this general framework there are usually multiple, overlapping, and frequently conflicting reasons for undertaking an evaluation. This multiplicity results from the many different perspectives of those who have a vested interest in the outcome of an evaluation.

For a typical high school moral education program, we can specify at least nine different groups of individuals likely to be interested in the outcome of a program evaluation: school-board members, administrators, program directors, program staff, evaluators, teachers, students, parents, and other community members. It is most unlikely that all these groups have a common set of expectations for the outcome of an evaluation. By virtue of their various relationships to the school, they will have a divergent set of aspirations concerning the content, dissemination, utilization, and eventual effect of a program evaluation.

To illustrate this point, let us explore a hypothetical case. Suppose that it has been decided that a particular program in a high school is to be evaluated. School-board members may wish to determine whether the extra expenditures required to continue the program can be justified. They may be most interested in obtaining data on the additional per-pupil expenditures required to achieve a specific goal, perhaps an average score increase of 10 points on some standardized test.

The principal and other administrators may share the school board's interest in a cost-benefit analysis. However, because they had initially supported the establishment of the program, they might hope that the evaluation will provide information that can be used to confirm the wisdom of their advocacy. Should the cost-benefit analysis not produce definitive, positive evidence, the administrators might turn to anecdotal materials.

The program director may be more interested in collecting sufficient data to support the position that the program should be expanded. The director might, for example, want to prove that the program is particularly effective in producing score increases for a subset of students, perhaps females or a particular minority group. The program's teaching staff may be convinced that the program is highly successful. From their viewpoint, evidence to support their perceptions may be detailed case studies documenting the most dramatic examples of the positive effect of the program on individual students. In addition, program staff may be interested in obtaining information which will allow them to make modifications in the program, with the intention of refining program operations for more effective achievement of program goals.

The evaluation staff, which might consist of one faculty member and several graduate students from a nearby university, may view the evaluation as an opportunity to assist the high school. However, at the same time they might be more interested in experimenting with a new data-collection technique, perhaps focused interviewing. In addition to providing a written report to the school, the evaluation team may want to produce an article describing the development and field testing of the interviewing technique for publication in a professional journal. They view the evaluation as an opportunity to conduct research, produce a scholarly publication, and thereby enhance their professional careers.

Other teachers in the high school, who do not participate in the program, may resent the expenditure of scarce funds. They may hope that the evaluation will be flawed and produce inconclusive results. Perhaps other teachers may furtively desire that the evaluation will demonstrate that the program is not attaining its goals and therefore should be discontinued. Despite reassurances to the contrary from program staff, students may suspect that the evaluation is a covert attempt to obtain additional assessment of their performance. Hence, they may be motivated to participate in the evaluation and perform as though it were some form of examination. Furthermore, some parents may share this misperception and encourage their children to "do well."

Finally, certain groups in the community, for example ethnic or racial minorities, may feel that the program operates to their disadvantage. Such opposition to the program may be based upon political grounds. Empirical data collected during the course of any evaluation will not sway their opinions. Regardless of the evidence produced by the evaluation, they may persist in their demands that the program either be modified or abolished altogether. If the evaluation results show that the program does have negative effects on the particular minority groups, they may use the evidence to support further their charges. On the other hand, should the results not support their claim, they may either ignore them or criticize them as being flawed.

All the expectations outlined above are certainly plausible in any high-school program evaluation. Furthermore, reality is usually much more complicated than our hypothetical case; perceptions concerning the purpose of program evaluation will vary within as well as among these groups. Rarely do all school-board members, or all teachers, or even all parents share common views on anything. This diversity of perceptions characterizes the political processes inherent in our local public school systems and is widely supported as a fundamental aspect of a democratic nation.

At this point, it will be useful to summarize by enumerating what we have encountered both in our fieldwork and literature review as the most commonly advanced reasons for program evaluations. We are certain that the list is not exhaustive, but we present it as further evidence of the vast diversity of opinions on this subject. Program evaluation may be undertaken to:

(1) measure the effects of a program against its specified goals;

(2) decide whether a program should be continued, expanded, modified, or terminated;

(3) justify a budget request;

(4) create additional support for a program;

(5) choose among alternative courses of action;

(6) function as a quality-control mechanism;

(7) field test theories;

(8) demonstrate the use of scientific management techniques;

(9) provide evidence to validate a program;

(10) provide feedback to program staff for minor adjustments in program operations;

(11) determine a basis for resource allocation; or

(12) establish procedures for identifying fiscal accountability.

In our experience, any one, and in some cases all, of the above purposes are acclaimed as legitimate reasons for undertaking evaluation. This list firmly establishes our earlier assertion that the purposes involved in undertaking evaluations are usually multiple, overlapping, and conflicting. At this point we can ask ourselves a troublesome question: If such diversity exists concerning the purposes of program evaluation, how is it possible to complete successfully a program evaluation?

In response to this question we introduce one of several major themes in this handbook. Recognizing that a diversity of opinions relevant to the purposes of a moral education program will necessarily exist within and among all groups, great efforts should be exerted to produce some minimal agreement on the expectations for its evaluation. Perhaps the most important step taken to insure a successful evaluation is to promote such agreement. If it cannot be achieved, it might be wise to forego the evaluation completely. It should be possible to arrive at some mutual understanding concerning the purpose of an evaluation. However, this is dependent upon agreement concerning the goals of the program itself, a topic to which we shall return in Chapter 4.

Chapter Two

TYPES OF
MORAL EDUCATION PROGRAMS

A definition of moral education

In order to be able to identify programs in "moral education," we needed some definition of the term "moral."[1] Such a definition is of course a complicated philosophical problem with a lengthy history — although we were surprised to find that it was rarely discussed in the literature on moral education. For our purposes, we defined it as referring to the issue of whether individuals, in making decisions about their own intentions or actions, take into account the needs and wishes of others as ends in themselves. This definition was formulated with several important points in mind:

(1) Morality is a matter of attitude and hence of predisposition or intention, as well as of action. Moral attitudes are not all necessarily carried out in action during any given period of observation, perhaps because the opportunities to do so do not arise or perhaps because of countervailing considerations during that time.

(2) The distinction between "needs" and "wishes" is meant to suggest that individuals do not always "want" what they "need," nor "need" what they "want."[2] Consequently, a person acting according to moral standards may sometimes disregard what another wants in order to do what the other is believed to need, and conversely may sometimes

---

[1]We consider "moral" to be synonymous, for all practical purposes, with "ethical."

[2]For this reason, we do not use the term "interests," which is ambiguous with respect to that distinction.

choose to act as another wishes even though that may not be what the other is believed to need. The choice of one or the other of these courses of action is a major moral problem, and obviously it involves the ability to know what the needs and wishes of others are and to make the distinction between them. For convenience, we will sometimes condense "needs and wishes" into the single term "well-being."

(3) Specifying that the needs and wishes of others be considered "as ends in themselves" is meant to exclude situations in which individuals strive to accommodate or please others merely as one way of attaining their own objectives. An interesting implication of this is that, as Hill and Wallace (1977) have suggested, the design of a moral education program, if it is to be consistent with its own premises, must "be sensitive to the concerns and interests of [its] potential users."

(4) Nevertheless, a particular decision can be morally acceptable even though it does not satisfy the needs or the wishes of specific other people or of others in general. All that is required is that the decision give due weight to those needs or wishes. How much weight to give to the (often conflicting) needs and wishes of various others in particular situations and how much to weigh all of them relative to one's own needs and wishes are problems that are of course at the heart of morality. However, we would not ordinarily say that a person's behavior was moral over the long term unless the person gave primacy to the needs or wishes of others on at least some occasions. A corollary of this is that patterns of behavior may be moral to varying degrees, according to the frequency with which the needs and wishes of others are given primacy in the decisions of the persons in question.

(5) "Others" may be individuals or groups of individuals. Societies and other social groups also have needs, which may be ultimately attributable to the needs (and wishes) of individuals for stable and satisfying relations with other individuals but which cannot necessarily be identified as the needs or wishes of any particular individual at any particular time.

A related problem, which seems not to have been discussed in the literature at all, is to define the "domain" of moral decisions, which would lead to a demarcation of the educational areas in which moral considerations would be appropriate. Are all attitudes and actions subject to moral considerations, or are there some which are merely "technical," "instrumental," or "esthetic," or which are matters of arbitrary preference, where the needs or wishes of others are simply not relevant? We tried for some time to find a satisfactory answer to this question, but in the end we concluded that it was impossible to identify any sorts of decisions to which moral considerations would in principle be inapplicable. It is in the nature of human existence that every decision has consequences for other people. This is admittedly a troubling conclusion, for it raises the specter of a tormented life in which every action is preceded by grave thought about its moral aspects; yet we do not see how this implication can be avoided. Perhaps one of the goals of a moral education program should be to help students develop principles for deciding when the moral dimensions of a problem, even though present, may properly be ignored.

In practice, a moral education program will probably concentrate on those decisions where the consequences for others are most important or most certain. Since many such decisions are part of the political and economic processes of the larger society — for example, laws have an intrinsically moral basis — instruction concerning them will often be located in the social studies, and moral education thus overlaps with civic education.[3] But it should be borne in mind (a) that it is not easy to know exactly what will ultimately prove to be "important" or how "certain" any effect is; (b) that importance and certainty vary with time and circumstances; and (c) that a great many decisions do not enter in any immediate way into the political or economic institutions yet have significant effects upon smaller circles of people.

Thus, we defined "programs in moral education" to mean deliberate efforts, within a school setting, to increase (a) students' abilities to consider the potential impact of their behavior on the well-being of others and (b) students' willingness to allow such considerations to affect their decisions despite potentially adverse effects upon themselves. It will be noted that, by this definition, a program in moral education would have both a cognitive and an affective component. On the cognitive side, the program would include an effort to cultivate the abilities to discern the needs and wishes of others and to "predict," to some extent, the effects of one's own actions on the lives of others. On the affective side, it would attempt to cultivate the desire to use these abilities in one's decision making even when one does not benefit from doing so in any calculated way. There is indeed general agreement among designers and observers of moral education programs that every such program should have these two elements, although of course the respective emphases they receive will vary from one program to another. Given our position on the domain of morality, we placed no limits on the subject areas in which a moral education program could appear, or on whether it would be taught as a separate subject or incorporated into the teaching of some other subject or subjects. However, a great many educational programs deal with moral issues to one degree or another, and of course we could not include all of them, so we restricted ourselves to those in which moral issues were, in our judgment, at least a moderately important element.

Implicit in this definition is the belief that it is probably impossible to specify in advance the morally correct decision for any class of problem

---

[3]For an argument that this overlap should be large and explicit, see Butts (1980).

situations. It is an enormously complicated task to identify the "others" involved (and there may be a very large number of them, in the present and in the future) and their needs and wishes and the weights to be assigned to them, and to determine the effects that one's action will have on all of this. Therefore, a moral education program will presumably have to focus on the *process* of decision making rather than on the product, on the reasons rather than on the substantive conclusions. This, too, is a matter of general agreement. It is a tactically wise approach to take as well, in view of the "heterogeneity of value commitments, life styles, and moral norms" and the "discrepancy between the professed ideals of the community as enunciated in the objectives of the school and tolerated behavior in the community" (Broudy, 1977) that a public school is likely to confront. Thus, we exclude from our definition efforts at indoctrination, in which students are urged to adopt certain moral stands without regard to the reasons for them. (This is not to say that moral reasoning, and perhaps even some substantive moral conclusions, may not become habitual, in the same way that most people eventually come to understand words and mathematical formulae without "thinking" about them.) We also decided to exclude moral education programs in religious schools, because we assumed the experience with them would not be generalizable to the public schools. But now, of course, we can only hope that others will fill in this gap that we have left. Finally, for administrative reasons we limited ourselves to programs being offered in public secondary schools in the United States, although there is considerable work of interest being done in elementary schools (see, e.g., Lipman and others, 1977) and at both elementary and secondary levels in Canada and Great Britain (Beck and others, 1972; Beck and others, 1976; Downey and Kelly, 1978; Wilson, 1972) and probably elsewhere as well.

Types of programs in moral education

We found a fairly large number of programs that met the criteria of our definition. They seemed to vary along six dimensions: Their origins or sources; their principal goals, purposes, or expected outcomes; their teaching strategies; the relative emphasis they gave to cognitive and affective components; their relative emphasis as between individual satisfaction and social obligation; and the nature of their concern for the relationship between actions and expressed values. We did not find programs that exemplified every possible combination of the "poles" of these dimensions, but there was considerable variation. The programs that we studied could be classified into four types, which were adapted from a typology devised by Superka and others (1976)[4] but in which we employed slightly different names: developmental, values clarification,

---

[4]Related typologies are given in Fenton (1977b) and in Hersh and others (1980).

actionist, and rationalist. Few operating programs fell neatly into a single category, but each program could be characterized as being predominantly of one type or another. The descriptions of the types which follow are based upon observations made in the pilot and field studies, documents produced by program developers, and discussions in the relevant literature.

Developmental. Programs of this type are probably the most widely taught and have almost certainly received more attention in both the academic-oriented and practitioner-oriented literature than those of any other type. The apparent reason for this is that they are most closely tied to an extensive body of psychological research and a theoretical framework which includes an explicit position concerning the criteria of morality. This foundation is particularly associated with the work of Lawrence Kohlberg and his associates and students of the Center for Moral Education at Harvard University (see especially Kohlberg, 1971, 1978; Kohlberg and Mayer, 1972). Building on earlier work by the Swiss psychologist Jean Piaget, Kohlberg hypothesized that individuals would go through certain stages of moral development, concomitant with their cognitive growth. In order to test this hypothesis, he devised a research procedure, the "Moral Judgment Interview," in which he described to respondents several moral dilemmas, asked them a set of questions about how they would deal with them or what they thought about them, and then scored their answers according to a standardized scheme. One of these dilemmas is shown on page 18, with the accompanying questions. After administering the interviews to people of different ages and sometimes to the same individuals repeatedly over a period of years, Kohlberg contended he had found that their answers would be classified into six modes of "moral reasoning," and that these modes did indeed constitute a set of successive "stages" of thought, because:

(1) They were "structured wholes" — i.e., organized and consistent ways of thinking about different kinds of moral problems.

(2) They formed an invariant sequence. The modes always followed each other in the same order during an individual's development, although most people did not reach the last mode and many did not reach the last two or three; a mode was never skipped over when its turn in the sequence came; and people who reached a given mode never returned to an earlier one.

(3) The sequence was "hierarchically integrated" — i.e., it represented a logical progression, in which each mode was both cognitively and philosophically more "adequate" than the one which preceded it, in the sense that it was able to handle a wider range of problems and to deal with them more satisfactorily. That was precisely why the modes did form a sequence. Drawing upon the earlier work of Jean Piaget, Kohlberg theorized that, as individuals matured, they were able to understand and use more

Figure 2.1: A Kohlberg Dilemma

In Europe, a woman was near death from a special kind of cancer. There was one drug that the doctors thought might save her. It was a form of radium that a druggist in the same town had recently discovered. The drug was expensive to make, but the druggist was charging ten times what the drug cost him to make. He paid $200 for the radium and charged $2,000 for a small dose of the drug. The sick woman's husband, Heinz, went to everyone he knew to borrow the money, but he could only get together about $1,000, which is half of what it cost. He told the druggist that his wife was dying and asked him to sell it cheaper or let him pay later. But the druggist said, "No, I discovered the drug and I'm going to make money from it." So Heinz got desperate and broke into the man's store to steal the drug for his wife.

Questions:
1. Should Heinz have done that? Was it actually wrong or right? Why?

2. Is it a husband's duty to steal the drug for his wife if he can get it no other way? Would a good husband do it?

3. Did the druggist have the right to charge that much when there was no law actually setting a limit to the price? Why?

   Questions 4a and b are asked if the interviewee says Heinz should steal the drug.

4. a) If the husband does not feel very close or affectionate to his wife, should he still steal the drug?

   b) Suppose it wasn't Heinz's wife who was dying of cancer but it was Heinz's best friend. His friend didn't have any money and there was no one in his family willing to steal the drug. Should Heinz steal the drug for his friend in that case? Why?

   Questions 5a and b are asked if the interviewee says Heinz should not steal the drug.

5. a) Would you steal the drug to save your wife's life?

   b) If you were dying of cancer but were strong enough, would you steal the drug to save your own life?

6. Heinz broke into the store and stole the drug and gave it to his wife. He was caught and brought before the judge. Should the judge send Heinz to jail for stealing or should he let him go free? Why?

differentiated and more complicated modes of reasoning and to discover the advantages they offered; consequently, individuals moved from one stage to the next higher one as soon as they had learned about it and had developed the cognitive skills needed to understand it. Kohlberg thus called his approach to moral education the "cognitive-developmental" approach (Kohlberg, 1971, 1978). A summary of the form of thought about moral problems characteristic of each of the six stages is given on page 20.

Kohlberg also held that, since the same sequence had been found in a number of different cultures, it was a "universal" pattern and therefore could serve as the basis for deliberate moral instruction without being subject to the charge of being "biased" toward one particular philosophical or religious viewpoint — a charge that, if true, might make it inappropriate for use in the public schools (Kohlberg and Mayer, 1972). On the other hand, the stages were said to move toward a single supreme virtue, that of justice, and so teaching them would avoid another possibly disabling charge of offering students mere "moral relativism."

Soon, Kohlberg and his students were experimenting with moral instruction based on this theory (Scharf, 1978b). The heart of this instruction was the classroom discussion of the moral dilemmas that Kohlberg had used in his research. The teachers' task in the discussion was to ensure that, when students expressed opinions about a moral problem, they would soon afterward hear an opinion expressed that used moral reasoning one stage beyond theirs; teachers might articulate this "plus-one" reasoning themselves or, preferably, identify students who had themselves reached a higher stage and encourage *them* to do so. Repeated exposure to higher-stage reasoning, together with increasing cognitive sophistication, would eventually bring students to understand the next higher stage, to perceive its superiority, and thus to adopt it for their own moral reasoning. The rate at which cognitive-moral development took place would thereby be accelerated, and at least some students would presumably reach higher stages than they would otherwise (Beyer, 1978; Wilson, 1972). The discussion could take place during periods specifically devoted to that purpose or in the context of the study of other subject matter (for which new dilemmas were sometimes written or were drawn from the particular subject matter — e.g., literature, history, or current events). Later, the approach was applied to the student guidance and counseling function (Mosher and Springhall, 1971), to a course in which students both discussed moral dilemmas and engaged in counseling peers and younger children (Mosher and Sullivan, 1978), and to a program in which discussions of moral dilemmas were integrated into a three-year sequence of English and social studies (Fenton, 1977a).

Figure 2.2: Summaries of the Forms of Thought
Characteristic of Kohlberg's Six "Stages of Moral Development"[a]

Preconventional stages

1. Punishment and obedience orientation
   The physical consequences of action for oneself determine its goodness or badness. Avoidance of punishment and unquestioning deference to power are valued insofar as they are beneficial to oneself.

2. The instrumental relativist orientation
   Right actions are those which instrumentally satisfy one's own needs. Human relations are chiefly a matter of reciprocity, interpreted in an immediate, pragmatic way: "you scratch my back and I'll scratch yours."

Conventional stages

3. Interpersonal concordance orientation
   Good behavior is that which pleases others and is approved by them, and it is conceived of in stereotyped terms of what the majority does or what it is "natural" to do. Good intentions ("he means well") influence the judgments of action for the first time. One can earn approval by being "nice."

4. Law and order orientation
   Right behavior consists of doing one's duty, showing respect for authority, and helping to maintain the social order for its own sake. Obedience to rules is important.

Postconventional or principled stages

5. Social-contract orientation
   Right action is defined in terms of general individual rights and standards which have been critically examined and agreed upon by the whole society. The diversity of personal values and opinions is recognized, and there is an emphasis upon procedural rules for reaching consensus. There is a corresponding emphasis upon the "legal point of view," but with a recognition of the possibility of changing the laws out of rational considerations of social utility. Outside the legal realm, freely arrived at agreements are the major elements of obligation.

6. Universal ethical principle orientation
   Right action is defined according to abstract, autonomously adopted ethical principles appealing to logical comprehensiveness, universality, and consistency. Basically, these principles are justice, the reciprocity and equality of human rights, and respect for the dignity of human beings as individual persons.

---

[a]Adapted from Porter and Taylor (1971).

Meanwhile, another element was added to some cognitive-developmental programs which transformed them into a force for change in the very structure of the school. From his experience in trying to implement the approach, Kohlberg concluded that student progression through the stages was often blocked by the organization of the school itself, which tended to exemplify conventional morality. Hence, he and others have made efforts to establish within the school a "community" made up of the teachers and students participating in the program and operating according to the principles of justice and equality that marked the highest stages of moral development. (In keeping with the premises of Kohlberg's theory, he called this a "just community," but others have used different terms.) In this "school within a school," teachers and students, acting as equals, would exercise powers of self-government as far as possible. It would thus both avoid the developmental restraints of the ordinary school and present students with more "realistic" and hence more motivating dilemmas (Wasserman, 1976). Presumably, it would also demand greater attention to the relationships between expressed moral choices and actions than the mere discussion of moral dilemmas did.

Kohlberg's approach to moral education has commanded great attention and respect because of its academic and theoretical origins and connections and the high quality of the research on which it was founded and which it has inspired; many people also find it appealing because of the sense of orderly progression toward a well defined goal that it lends to instruction in what is otherwise a rather nebulous area. But it has also been the target of many criticisms. The claims for its universality and for other aspects of the theory are based, it is said, on rather skimpy evidence (Simpson, 1974); developmental models other than Kohlberg's are at least as sound, even if they cannot so readily be made to serve as the basis of instruction (Hall and Davis, 1975; Hoffman, 1970). It has been suggested that the stages cannot really be distinguished from each other as discrete modes of thought (Keasey, 1974; Locke, 1979). Even a supporter of Kohlberg's theory has argued that stages 5 and 6 are not hierarchically related to each other and ought not be regarded as part of the developmental-stage sequence (Gibbs, 1979). There is some question —apparently even in Kohlberg's mind — about the very existence of a stage 6 (Butts, 1980; Gibbs, 1977),[5] and stage 5 may occur so

---

[5] One of the difficulties in discussing Kohlbergian programs is that the stage definitions — as well as the dilemmas, interview questions, and scoring techniques — are frequently changed, with the changes sometimes being reported only orally or in unpublished materials, so that one is not always sure of having the "latest information." In this discussion, we have limited ourselves to statement which can be verified and further explored in materials likely to be readily accessible to the readers.

rarely as to make it pointless to try to teach for it.[6] There is evidence that individuals do not necessarily prefer a stage higher than their own even when they can understand it (Keasey, 1974); if that is the case, it might render the "plus-one" teaching strategy futile. Doubts have also been raised as to whether each stage is more "adequate" than the preceding one. As Locke (1979) has pointed out, decision making at the higher stages may well be more *difficult* than at the lower stages, because the higher-stage thinker takes a wider range of people and eventualities into account; and while thinking at the higher stages may be more "sophisticated," sophistication per se is not necessarily morally to the "simple moral consciousness" that has been celebrated by some writers and philosophers. Nor is the character of reasoning at one stage qualitatively better than at a preceding stage; indeed, progression through the Kohlberg stages may not rely on reasoning at all but rather on the holistic more or less intuitive grasp of a set of attitudes.

Kohlberg's theory has also been challenged on logical and philosophical grounds. "Justice" in and of itself is not a sufficient basis for making decisions. Deciding what is "just" in a given situation requires a determination of exactly which circumstances are "relevant" to that situation and how each of them is to be evaluated, and this "opens up obvious possibilities for alternative emphases in morality" even within the constraints of "justice" (Peters, 1971). Kohlberg argues that his theory concerns forms of thought, not action, and that moral thinking at any one stage is compatible with a wide range of actions; and to argue otherwise would lead to the necessity for specifying what kind of action is "moral," which would in turn undermine the claim that the theory is not tied to any particular culture (Locke, 1979).[7] Yet, if a mode of thought does *not* limit action, one may wonder what its value is. Moreover, justice is not universally accepted as the supreme virtue, even within Western culture; arguments have been made for freedom and love, among others, as the occupants of that status, and they sometimes conflict with justice (Plattner, 1979).[8] There are those who doubt that

---

[6]On the other hand, by the definition of "morality" which we used (see above, pp. 13-14) stages 1 and 2 do not qualify as "moral" thought at all, because they do not take into account the needs and wishes of others "as ends in themselves" but only in relation to one's own satisfactions. E.V. Sullivan (1977) has remarked that, by its classification of all thought about moral problems into one stage or another, the developmental approach seems to negate the possibility of "moral failure"; — i.e., of immorality. (See also Gibbs and others, 1976).

[7]Nevertheless, Kohlberg does seem on occasion to use the commission or non-commission of specific acts — such as stealing, cheating on a test, or engaging in a protest demonstration — as evidence with which to validate his theory (Kohlberg, 1970, 1971, 1979).

[8]Kohlberg frequently acknowledges his debt to John Rawls' book *A Theory of Justice*, as the source of his understanding of the concept. But Plattner (1979) also subjects the reasoning in that book to trenchant criticism.

there is any single supreme virtue at all. Finally, the suspicion has been raised that, in theory and especially in classroom practice, Kohlberg's "stages" are in effect expressions of different political ideologies (Bennett and Delattre, 1978; Hoffman, in press); thus, to teach that the modes of thought are hierarchically ordered would be to express covert preferences among these ideologies.

The teaching practices associated with developmental programs of moral education have also been criticized, even by some who nevertheless support the introduction of such programs. The dilemmas that are used for discussion purposes seem often to be extremely simple in structure; this may be useful for pedagogical purposes (Beyer, 1978), but it may give students the idea that moral problems are much less complex than they actually are (Fraenkel, 1978). Little concern seems to have been given to the selection of types of dilemmas that would be most suitable for students reasoning at different stages or varying in age or other characteristics (Fraenkel, 1978). The teacher who is guiding the discussion of moral dilemmas is supposed to avoid "assuming an expository or authoritarian role" or "putting students down," so that students will not be deterred from expressing their opinions freely and interacting with one another (Beyer, 1978); yet the teacher who follows that advice runs the risk of conveying the message that "all modes of moral thought are equally good," which would tend toward the "moral relativism" that Kohlberg sought to avoid and might even discourage students from striving toward "higher" stages. Even without worrying about that, the task of guiding the discussions places great demands on the teachers; as Fraenkel (1978) has commented, to expect teachers to

> listen to several responses of each student, figure out what stage of reasoning these responses suggest, and then either frame an appropriate "one stage higher" response during on-going class discussion, or mix the students with others who are reasoning one stage higher...seems to be asking an awful lot from busy classroom teachers.

Scharf, an advocate of cognitive-developmental programs of moral education concedes that most of these programs "were conducted...by university professors or doctoral candidates....The philosophic complexity of the Kohlberg system raises the question of whether the approach only works in the hands of Stage 5 teachers selected from good university graduate programs" (Scharf, 1978a).

The "just community" also has its problems. It may be viewed as "intimidating" by students, as they become aware that their teachers and some of their fellow students know of a "'higher' morality which was better than theirs" and as they experience a "tremendous pressure to choose the 'right' side," even when they do not understand why it is "right" or "better" (Zalaznick, 1980). Indeed, the very notion that there are "higher" and "lower" modes of moral thought implies "an elitism

that is difficult to disguise" (Flowers, 1978) and that appears to be inconsistent with the principle of equality — derived, ironically, from the
principle of justice — on which the "just community" is based (Scharf,
1978b, pp. 216-217).

Values Clarification. Like the cognitive-developmental approach to
moral education, values clarification arose out of the work of one man, in
this case Louis E. Raths, who taught in the School of Education at New
York University. Raths had been deeply affected by the behaviors he had
seen abroad during World War II, and he detected signs that youth in the
United States were acquiring characteristics that he thought had been
partly responsible for the rise of Nazism. Specifically, he found that "far
too many children in the schools" were "apathetic, flighty, uncertain,
inconsistent, drifters, overconformers, overdissenters, and poseurs"
(Raths and others, 1966). The reason for this, he believed, was that young
people did not have a clear set of personal values to which they could
commit themselves. He defined a "value" — not altogether explicitly
—as a mental predisposition that met seven criteria: (1) it had been freely
chosen by an individual, (2) from among alternatives and (3) after
thoughtful consideration of the consequences of each of the alternatives; it was (4) prized and cherished, (5) publicly affirmed, and (6) acted
upon, and (7) it constituted a pattern of action in the individual's life
(Raths and others, 1966). It was in particular the concern with the "consequences of alternatives" that led us to include values clarification
among the types of moral education.

Raths and several associates — especially Merrill Harmin, Sidney B.
Simon, and later Howard Kirschenbaum — developed a series of pedagogical techniques to stimulate the process of value formation among
students, and this set of techniques soon came to identify the values-
clarification "movement." The two principal original methods were the
"clarifying response" and the "value sheet." In the former, the teacher
responds to a student's comment with a remark or a question that would
provoke the student "to look at his life and his ideas and to think about
them." (Raths and others, 1966). The response might be something as
simple as "What do you mean by that?" or "You don't seem to care much
about that." The value sheet was a series of questions on a topic drawn
from current news events or from the subject matter of a course, to
which students were asked to respond in writing; the questions were
designed to induce them to articulate the meaning of the topic for their
own lives and thus, again, to examine their values. Students might then
discuss their reponses among themselves, in small groups, or some of the
answers might be read aloud (anonymously) to the whole class, or the
teacher might return the sheets to the students with marginal comments.
A number of other techniques were also suggested, and teachers were

encouraged to devise their own as well.[9] As values clarification spread, some of its practitioners adapted techniques that had become popular in encounter groups and similar settings, and classrooms in which it was being used sometimes took on a "games" atmosphere.

Unlike the supporters of the cognitive-developmental approach, values clarification advocates at first tended to discourage extended classroom discussions because it was feared that students would be argumentative and defensive or would yield too easily to suggestions from their teachers or peers; and in any case, they said, the formation of values was a process that had to go on privately, not in a group. The values-clarification technique emphasized brief, almost random, encounters between a teacher and a student, and teachers were even given tips on how to break off the conversation after two or three exchanges. Later, though, this attitude was relaxed, and period-length discussions involving an entire class were not uncommon. Since clarifying questions were intended to suggest to students that there might be alternatives to their way of thinking, and since moral dilemmas were one source of "provocative" questions, and since teachers in both the cognitive-developmental and the values-clarification approaches were urged not to criticize students for what they said, lest discussion be dampened, the actual proceedings in classrooms using the two approaches might not always be easily distinguished (Kirschenbaum, 1977b); Kohlberg, in Simon and Kirschenbaum, 1973, p. 63). Even the idea of a "just community" has been used as a way of creating a school-wide stimulus to thought about values.

There are some differences, however. Values clarification puts great stress on the premise that values are a matter of personal choice; it does not posit any supreme virtue such as justice, nor does it make any assumptions about stages or direction of growth. In part at least, this grew out of Raths' concern to avoid anything that might smack of indoctrination; he was also convinced that a program in values education could not be successful in the public schools unless it refrained from advocating any particular, substantive value position. Second, because of its emphasis on the importance of values to personal behavior, the subject matter of values-clarification techniques is more likely to be drawn from everyday events and from the students' own immediate concerns, rather than from abstract or hypothetical problems. Third, as indicated by the seven criteria of a value, it takes the position that one must act on one's values; as long as a predisposition remains purely mental, it is but a value "indicator," not a full-fledged value. The action,

_____

[9]Kirschenbaum later became director of the National Humanistic Education Center, in Saratoga Springs, NY, which produces a large volume of material for use by practitioners of values clarification and also conducts workshops for teachers and others interested in the approach.

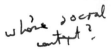

furthermore, must be "constructive in the social context" as well as satisfying to the individual (Kirschenbaum, 1977b; Kirschenbaum and others, 1977). Fourth, writings on values clarification make frequent reference to the "skills" of valuing, to "learning how" to value (Kirschenbaum and others, 1977; Raths and others, 1966), although the materials do not seem to deal with these skills any more than Kohlbergian programs include instruction in "reasoning." These differences are nicely summarized in the following statement by two of the people most closely identified with values clarification (Harmin and Simon, 1973):

> The main task of [values clarification] is not to identify and transmit the "right" values, but to help a student clarify his own values so he can obtain the values that best suit him and his environment; so he can adjust himself to a changing world; and so he can play an intelligent role in influencing the way the world changes.

The attractiveness of values clarification probably lies in its simplicity and ease of implementation and its overt abstinence from any substantive moral position. But of course it has come in for its share of criticism. It is frequently pointed out that, unlike the latter, it was not derived from psychological theory of research, and as a result it acquired an ad hoc air, without any coherent framework to guide a teacher's selection of methods or materials.[10] Not all predispositions that would ordinarily be called "values" meet the criteria set forth by Raths and his associates; for example, some values are absorbed from the family during early childhood, and the fact that they are not "freely chosen" does not make them any less values (Lockwood, 1976).[11] As we said earlier, it is not always possible to perform actions implementing every personal value in any finite period of time (see also Stewart, 1975). Moreover, values clarification, it has been said, underestimates the complexity of the relationships between thought and action. It seems likely that many different kinds of action are consistent with a given value; but if that is the case, it is difficult to know whether a particular value is being acted upon, and the claim of values clarification that it reduces uncertainty is weakened (Lockwood, 1976).

---

[10]Kirschenbaum (1977a) has reviewed the research that has subsequently been done on values clarification. However, it is rather vaguely described; most of it appeared in the form of graduate dissertations; the results were often mixed or inconclusive; and there is no indication that any of it led to changes in the procedures suggested for the use of values-clarification techniques.

[11]Kirschenbaum (1973) has conceded the difficulties with Raths' seven criteria. "It would be better," he wrote, "to speak of the *processes* of *valuing* rather than of the criteria of values. These processes are feeling, thinking, communicating, choosing, and acting. There may be others..." His reformulation did not satisfy the critics, and in any event other writings of the supporters of values clarification continued to refer to the seven criteria (e.g., see Kirschenbaum and others, 1977).

26

The avoidance of value positions and the absence of a theoretical basis in either psychology or philosophy are interpreted by some to mean that values clarification does not foster student growth, the accumulation of knowledge or understanding, or increased sophistication of moral judgment (Harrison, 1976). Similarly, the strictures against any sort of "imposition" of values, which supporters treat as one of the strengths of values clarification, is taken by others to mean that values are being presented merely as matters of arbitrary personal preference, to which no principles of selection need be or should be applied (Lockwood, 1976). Others have charged that, like cognitive-developmental moral education, values clarification has certain values covertly built into it — in this case, whatever the opposites of "apathy, flightiness, uncertainty," etc., are (Stewart, 1975), or simply "narcissistic self-gratification" as the supreme value (Bennett and Delattre, 1978).

Actionist. This type of program had more diffuse sources than the two that have been discussed so far. Designers of actionist programs cite the idea of "learning by doing" that has been associated with John Dewey and more recently with Ralph Tyler, and the stages of identity formation described by Erik Erikson, as well as Kohlberg's work in moral development and particularly its application by Mosher and Sprinthall (Hedin and Schneider, 1978). They have also been influenced by the writings of social scientists such as Urie Bronfenbrenner (1970) and James Coleman (Panel on Youth, 1974), who were concerned about the transition from school to the adult world and either showed how it was done in other societies or suggested how it might be improved in the U.S. The distinctive inference that they draw from this background is that young people need opportunities for "significant interaction with the environment" in order to achieve maximum growth. The school could not provide such opportunities: it was regarded as an isolated and "artificial" setting, containing only a limited range of roles, with students playing a subordinate part. Consequently, to find these opportunities, students had to be sent out into the "real world" of the community and the larger society. A precedent for such "experiential learning" had been set by Outward Bound programs in which students are challenged to cope with wilderness conditions, but actionist supporters believe effective encounters can be had not only in the wilderness but also in the cities and towns where students live.

In terms of their relevance to moral education, the implication of actionist programs is that students were not to face contrived or historical moral problems nor dwell upon their own problems and those of their peers, but instead they would deal with the real problems that the adults in their own communities were facing every day. Furthermore, because students were engaged in activities that had "real" consequences for other people (rather than leading merely to grades on a report card), moral problems would take on a seriousness that they could not have in the classroom. "'Hands-on' experiences in moral development," it has been argued, are just as useful and important as they are in the learning of occupational skills (Riles, 1975). In a sense, actionist programs can be seen as an extension of the "just community" that grew out of developmental programs: a way to allow students — if not force them — to come to grips with real moral problems. The drawback of the just community, from this point of view, was that it still lacked some elements of "reality," in that it remained within the school context and was based upon a degree of egalitarianism not likely to be found elsewhere. On the other hand, it had the advantage of being able to integrate practice and study, of creating a situation in which moral problems were not only raised but brought to closure in an explicit fashion. In order to afford similar opportunities, many advocates of actionist programs urge that the program include time for classroom discussion of the moral problems that arise in the students' outside activities (e.g., Conrad and Hedin, 1977).

Actionist programs tend to stress the affective side of moral education probably more than any other types. Program rationales make frequent reference to the development of empathy and a sense of responsibility as being among the main outcomes of having to work interdependently with other people in order to produce some result. The affective aspects of morality are seen as the source of motivation for acquisition of the cognitive skills. However, the practical demands of the activities are also believed to have important cognitive results.

The National Commission on Resources for Youth, one of the main organizational supporters of such programs,[12] has classified the kinds of activities in which students in actionist programs might engage into the following types: (1) Helping service to others, in which students meet "face to face with other people in a helping relationship." (2) Community service, in which students assist a neighborhood or community organization. (3) Social action, in which they seek to bring about a specific institutional change such as a new law or the establishment of a service facility. (4) Community internships, in which they are placed individually with adults at their work places (Kohler and Dollar, 1978). Although actionist programs tend to have a natural affinity for voluntary, governmental, and non-profit organizations, business firms also are loci for student placements. In the usual case, one person at the placement site is asked to assume responsibility for enhancing the educational effects of the students' activities and for supervising them to some degree. Where students are working as a group to accomplish a goal, a teacher may have that task. In any of these cases, the actionist program

---

[12]Another important organization has been the Center for Youth Development and Research at the University of Minnesota. There is also an Association for Experiential Education, made up largely of actionist-program practitioners.

may take the form of an entire course in itself, or even the entire program of a student for some period of time, or it may be a required or optional part of a course, or it may be a co-curricular activity, with or without credit. In some instances, students may be paid for the work they do, either by an employer or through a federal program such as the Youth Employment Demonstration Projects Act.

Actionist programs of course have their own problems. There are no theoretical or empirical grounds for determining what will be an appropriate kind of activity for any given student or group of students. When placements have been made, they sometimes turn out to consist of little more than routine labor, or on the other hand they may demand more than students are able to give. Particularly in the case of individual placements, the logistics of transporting students to and from sites have sometimes been formidable; or, if students are given the responsibility of getting themselves there and back, it can be expensive and time-consuming. Placement supervisors who are able and willing to act as "supplementary teachers" may be hard to find, and they may not always have the same perception of their functions as the school does; and in any event, maintaining communication with them can be difficult. Partly for such reasons, the number of suitable placements available in a community may not be very large; and a school which operates an actionist program involving a substantial number of students over a fairly long period of time may find that it is exhausting the placement possibilities.

A common anxiety of those responsible for actionist programs is that they can easily slip into becoming small-scale vocational-education or career-preparation programs, since the aims of the latter are more concrete and may well be of greater interest to placement supervisors and to the students themselves (cf. Hedin and Conrad, 1979). It is easy enough — if not indeed positively appealing — for all concerned to stick to what is known and tangible and neglect the nebulous, complex, indeterminate, perhaps even embarrassing, problems of morality. Classroom discussions are supposed to guard against this eventuality; but no clear guidelines have been worked out for proper use of classroom time in actionist programs, and it is in the very nature of these programs that they tend to look upon time in the classroom as "wasted."

Rationalist. This approach is probably more closely connected than the others to the traditional pedagogical philosophy and method of the U.S. educational system. Perhaps for that reason, it lacks any elaborated rationale for its activities. The underlying assumptions appear to be that the superiority of rational procedures for, e.g., settling disputes is self-evident and that consequently students who acquire a sound cognitive understanding of these procedures will use them. The major organizations which have produced rationalist programs have tended to focus upon the law and legal institutions, as the most visible manifestations of "rational" methods of resolving political, social, and economic conflicts, and they have drawn heavily upon the legal profession for guidance and assistance.[13] The programs have also been closely linked with more or less conventional kinds of "civic" education, and their pedagogical methods have relied chiefly on reading materials and films and filmstrips for students and teachers, field trips to relevant places, and visits to the classroom by people active in one aspect or another of the legal system. One of the organizations, the Constitutional Rights Foundation, also makes use of peer- and cross-age teaching and classroom simulations of trials and hearings.

The engagement of rationalist programs with moral issues is surprisingly tenuous. Their goal statements do refer, for example, to increasing "a person's capacity and inclination to act knowledgeably, effectively, and responsibly," and to encouraging "a sense of fairness in social interactions and a respect for the rights of others" (Law in a Free Society, n.d.). Teachers' guides for some of the programs include exercises in values clarification and in dilemmas for discussion obviously inspired by the moral-development approach; indeed, Kohlberg has played a part in the development of some of the rationalist programs. But these techniques, and the issues they are concerned with, occupy a distinctly subsidiary position in the program. One might expect more than that. In a sense, laws are an embodiment of the moral views of society; and the concept of "justice," which is central to Kohlberg's theory of moral development, is also one of the most important aspects of a legal system. Yet inspection of the curriculum materials and visits to instructional sites make it clear that moral issues are less of a concern in programs of this type than in any of the others. Perhaps because of their origins and the context of their development, they place primary emphasis upon cognitive knowledge of how the legal system works, together with some effort at promoting "positive attitudes" toward the system and those who operate it. They exhibit little inclination to explore the concept of justice; rather, they seem to take it for granted that it is present in the U.S. legal system (which is sometimes referred to as "the justice system"). While the system's defects may be pointed out and even brought to the forefront for discussion, there appears to be no systematic consideration of what makes them "defects" — i.e., of the moral criteria by which a legal system might be evaluated. The "justice" in these programs sometimes seems to bear little relationship to the "justice" in developmental programs.

The chart on page 31 summarizes the features of the four types of moral education programs in terms of the dimensions mentioned earlier.

---

[13]We did learn of one rationalist program that was devoted entirely to ethical philosophical reasoning, with little or no legal content. This was the "Philosophy in the Classroom" program developed by Matthew Lipman of Montclair State College (NJ) (Lipman and others, 1977). However, this program has not been designed for or implemented at the secondary level.

Figure 2.3: Characteristics of Four Types of Moral-Education Programs

Dimension	Program Type			
	Development	Values Clarification	Actionist	Rationalist
Origins/sources	Research and theoretical formulations of Piaget and Kohlberg	Observations of Raths	Inferences drawn from Dewey, Erickson, Tyler, Kohlberg Outward Bound programs	Concern over students' lack of information, declining ethical standards, rising delinquency rates
Expected outcomes[a]	Advancement to higher stage of moral thought	Purposive action consistent with values	Ability to deal with "real" moral problems	Better understanding of the legal system, greater willingness to act within the law
Major pedagogical strategies	Discussion of moral dilemmas; organization of "just community"	Questions and comments designed to promote examination of values	Performance of services in the community	Traditional methods, such as readings, films, field trips, classroom visits
Cognitive/affective emphasis	Primarily cognitive	Primarily affective	Primarily affective	Primarily cognitive
Individual/social emphasis	Social obligations	Individual satisfactions	Social obligations	Individual participation a social obligation
Action/value relationship	Values important regardless of effect on actions	Values must be displayed in action	Values are formed through action	Noncommittal

[a]Only those outcomes pertinent to the moral aspects of programs are included here.

Chapter Three

DESIGNING AN EVALUATION

In this chapter we turn to the problems of designing an evaluation of a moral education program. Our discussion is relevant to any one or a combination of the four types of programs discussed in the previous chapter. After pointing out the importance of doing an exploratory study, we discuss several basic concepts pertinent to analyzing causal relationships. We then introduce the elements of the classic experimental design and indicate why this design is not usually workable. Finally, we introduce several variations of the experimental design, referred to as quasi-experiments, that are especially appropriate for evaluating moral education programs.

Exploratory studies

Evaluators of any moral education program should first conduct an exploratory study, before launching into the program, especially if they are not familiar with its components and the setting in which the program is to be conducted. There are two components in such a study. First, one should review the relevant educational and social-science literature. Fortunately, the task of conducting a literature review today can be greatly facilitated by computer searches of bibliographic data bases containing citations to and abstracts of current professional and scientific literature. The Educational Research Information Center (ERIC) data base is the most appropriate place to begin a literature review of materials relevant to evaluation of moral education programs. Access to the abstracts and citations in the ERIC file can be obtained readily during an on-line session by searching with substantive key words. A typical search of ERIC costs no more than $20 to $30. Searches can be conducted at most large academic and public libraries. (See Appendix C for a brief description of ERIC.) One should also become familiar with _Standards for Evaluation of Educational Programs, Projects, and Materials_ (Joint Committee on Standards, 1981), which was developed by a committee representing the major professional associations concerned with educational evaluation and which sets forth generally accepted criteria of quality and integrity.

The second major component of an exploratory study is field observation of the program in action. Here the investigator should observe classroom and other program activities, and interview students, teachers, and other participants. In carrying out these activities, the investigator should maintain a flexible and rather open-ended schedule to permit sufficient latitude to pursue unanticipated and promising leads. The purpose of this kind of investigation is to develop a better understanding of the program, as a basis for decisions about data-collection procedures, evaluation design, and hypotheses for subsequent testing.

Problems of design

The purpose of evaluation, like that of all research, is to discover relationships among variables. Variables are observations or measurements of individuals — e.g., students, teachers, parents — or groups of individuals — e.g., classes, schools, or government agencies. They are called "variables" because they are observations or measurements on which people or groups vary; for example, they may vary by age, grade-point average, or moral status. One, a relationship among variables that is of particular interest, is known as "causality." This is the relationship between what are called "independent variables," or causes, and "dependent variables," or effects. Social scientists generally agree that three conditions must be satisfied in order to infer a causal relationship between an independent and a dependent variable: concomitant variation, time order of occurrence, and elimination of other possible causes (Selltiz and others, 1976).

Concomitant variation means that the cause and the effect vary together: Whenever the independent variable increases (or decreases), the dependent variable increases (or decreases). For example, suppose we hypothesize that a new instructional program in mathematics will produce greater gains in scores on a standardized achievement test than conventional teaching methods. In this example, the independent variable is the type of mathematics instruction to which the students are exposed. This independent variable has only two categories, the new instructional program and the conventional teaching methods. The dependent variable could be the score that each student received on a

34

mathematics test. There are many categories here, ranging from the lowest to the highest possible score. We arrange for the use of the new instructional program in some classes but not in others. At the end of the semester, if students in the classes exposed to the new instructional techniques score higher than students in the traditional classes, we have evidence (though not necessarily conclusive evidence) that the new program and mathematics knowledge are "causally" related.

Time order of occurrence, the second condition, refers to the fact that a cause must precede the effect in time order. In our example, this condition can be satisfied in two possible ways. First, we might administer the test at the beginning of the course to measure the initial differences in mathematical achievement between students taking the conventional course and those enrolled in the new program. Alternatively, students could be assigned to the traditional or new program classes using an assignment procedure which allows us to assume that they did not differ in either their mathematical abilities or their prior knowledge of mathematics. We refer to this as using the research design to control for the possible effects of other independent variables.

Satisfying the conditions of concomitant variation and time order is possible in most evaluations, but the third condition, eliminating other possible causal explanations, is more troublesome. In evaluation research we usually want to test the hypothesis that a program will produce a specific outcome, but we frequently find it very difficult to employ a design that will convincingly eliminate all other possible causes. In a very real sense, this is an impossible task, for theoretically there are an infinite number of other possible causes. In addressing this problem the knowledge, skill, and judgment of the investigator are of paramount importance. A sound theoretical framework from which one derives hypotheses concerning causal relationships, combined with effective utilization of design features, will enable the investigator to make a convincing case for eliminating most other plausible independent variables.

Experimental designs

In the textbooks, an ideal evaluation design is said to look something like this: The (preferably very large) group of students who are to be the subjects of the evaluation is divided into two parts, an experimental or treatment group and a control or comparison group. The students are assigned randomly to one group or the other, to assure that there are no systematic differences between them at the outset.

There are many different ways to accomplish random assignment to experimental and control groups. The simplest procedure in this case is as follows:

1. make a list of the names of all students who will participate in the evaluation, i.e., be members of either experimental or control groups (the order of the names on this list is irrelevant);

2. number the names consecutively, starting with one;
3. pick any starting point in a table of random numbers (Rand Corporation, 1955) and use all succeeding numbers in the table to choose students' numbers from the list for placement in the experimental group until half the students are so assigned; and
4. place all remaining students in the control group. This procedure insures that each student is equally likely to be assigned to either group.

A measure is taken of all students' original status in relevant respects (in the present case, it would be some measure having to do with their moral status). If they have been truly randomly assigned, the measure will show that the two groups have the same status (after making due allowance for the inevitable measurement and sampling errors). Incidentally, the random assignment allows us to assume that the students do not differ on any other variables as well. The control group then receives exactly the same educational program that it would have received if no evaluation were going on. The treatment group also receives the same educational program that it would have received, except of course that it receives the treatment as well — e.g., the moral education program (presumably in place of something else that it would otherwise have received and which the control group *is* receiving). If the treatment group includes more than one class, all the classes receive exactly the same moral education program (and exactly the same everything else, too). At the end of the program, the program-relevant measure is administered again to both groups, and the gain from beginning to end shown by the treatment group minus the gain from beginning to end shown by the control group represents the program's accomplishment.

Figure 3.1 illustrates this true experimental model as it might be applied to a moral education program. Students are randomly assigned either to the experimental class or the control class. The observations or measures taken on students in both groups before the program starts are called the premeasurement, producing scores A and C in Figure 3.1.[1] (We will discuss the nature of these observations in Chapter 4.) The experimental students then participate in some other program which is comparable but does not contain a moral education component. A traditional civics or social-science course is frequently used for the control group. At the completion of the program, students in both sections are then postmeasured, using a procedure parallel to that used as a pretest, producing scores B and D in the figure. If the value of B

---

[1]We use the terms "premeasure" and "postmeasure" in this discussion as shorthand references to any type of data collection. We do not mean to imply the exclusive use of paper-and-pencil tests or indeed of any tests at all.

minus A is greater than the value of D minus C, the program is considered a success.[2]

Technically speaking, the premeasures are not required for a true experiment. If the random assignment is correctly executed, an analysis of the postmeasure is a sufficient test. However, premeasurement may sensitize the students to the process and cause a difference in postmeasurements. The possibility of bias caused by premeasurement can be explored by using two control groups, one being measured and the other not.

Figure 3.1: True Experiment for Moral Education Program Evaluation

	Premeasure	**Postmeasure**
Experimental Class	A	B
Control Class	C	D

As portrayed in Figure 3.2 there are three groups and five scores for comparison. Now students are randomly assigned to one of three groups. Premeasurements are taken for the experimental and first control group only; postmeasures are taken for all three groups. At the end of the program, we proceed with the analysis as follows: First we compare E with B and D. If these scores are not different, we can assume that pretesting does not cause any bias. We can then proceed with our analysis of the difference between B minus A and D minus C as before.

Analyses with the experimental design can be further extended by including additional experiments and control groups. Let us take one further example to show an extension with three experimental groups. Suppose it is claimed that developmental programs are more effective if they combine sessions in which the hypothetical moral dilemmas are

---

[2]The reader might well ask several questions at this point. First, how much of a difference is worth paying attention to? This is both a legitimate and very important issue. However, in order to maintain the continuity of our discussion of the experiments design, we shall take up this point later in Chapter 5. The reader might also ask about the possibility that the postmeasures scores might be lower than the premeasure scores. Alternatively, the control group might produce greater gains than the experimental group. Unfortunately, this happens all too frequently. It usually indicates that there are serious problems with the specification and measurement of program goals or objectives. Alternatively and less likely, it could mean that the program is producing exactly the opposite of its intentions. To facilitate our discussion, we shall keep our examples simple at this point and return to those problems as well later in the chapter.

Figure 3.2: True Experiment with Two Control Groups

	Premeasure	Postmeasure
Experimental Class	A	B
Control Class #1	C	D
Control Class #2	No Test	E

Figure 3.3: True Experiment with Multiple Groups

	Premeasure	Postmeasure
Experimental Class #1: Moral Discussion Groups Only	A	B
Experimental Class #2: Just Community Only	C	D
Experimental Class #3: Moral Discussion Groups and Just Community	E	F
Control Class #1	G	H
Control Class #2	No Test	I

discussed in regular weekly meetings of ɩe just community. We could explore this claim with an experimental design including five groups —three experimental and two control, as depicted in Figure 3.3.

Again, students are randomly assigned, but this time each student has equal probability of being placed in one of five groups. Students in experimental class 1 participate only in the guided discussions of the moral dilemmas; students in experimental class 2 participate only in just community meetings; and those in experimental class 3 participate in both the discussions and the meetings. Both premeasures and postmeasures are taken for students in all experimental classes and control group 1; only postmeasures are taken for those in control group 2.

We can now extend our analysis to include a number of questions. First, we examine the possible bias of premeasurement by comparing I with B, D, F, and H. If we conclude there is little or no such bias, we proceed by comparing the difference between the value of H minus G with the values of B minus A, D minus C, and F minus E. If the latter three differences are greater than the first, we conclude that the developmental program is a success. However, we continue the analysis to determine whether F minus E is greater than both B minus A and D minus C. If so, we conclude that the combination of moral-dilemma discussions and just-community meetings is more effective than either program component alone. Incidentally, the single comparison between B minus A and D minus C would also reveal which of the two program components was more effective.

It should be clear by now that the basic design of the true experiment can be extended almost ad infinitum by adding more experimental and control groups. For example, if we had some reason to suspect that pretest bias might only affect students exposed to a particular program component such as moral-dilemma discussion, we could add another control group with no pretesting but with exposure to the discussions. It should also be pointed out that the experimental design could be extended further by testing at several different intermediate points during the course of the program, thus giving rise to even more comparisons for testing hypotheses.

True experiments are rarely possible in school settings. Lee Cronbach, the distinguished educational psychologist and evaluation specialist, has enunciated a principle that is the evaluation version of Murphy's Law. It is that "controls break down" (Cronbach, 1978). For administrative reasons, it is rarely possible to assign students to one group or another at random. Whatever method of assignment is used, the composition of experimental and control groups will not remain constant, anyway; scheduling problems require that students be shifted from one group to the other in mid-program, new students come in and some of the original ones leave, others are absent for substantial periods of time. New teaching methods are being tried out in, say, the social studies, and some of the moral-education subjects are participating in that experiment as well, while others are not. Two different classes can never receive the same treatment even in the same program: the availability of materials (or of action-placement sites or classroom visitors) differs, the time of day differs, above all the teachers differ. Students in the control group interact with students in the experimental group and may even read some of the materials being used. Any experienced educator can add a dozen more contingencies to this list.

Quasi-experimental design

Cronbach's advice, in the circumstances that have been described, is not to abandon the hope of evaluation but to tailor the design to the facts of life and even take advantage of them, by combining experimental and naturalistic approaches. If students cannot be randomly assigned, one must at least learn as much as possible about those who are in the two groups. The initial measure of their moral status (or preferably, as we shall discuss later, several measures) will show how and how much they differ. In addition, one ought to learn something about their socioeconomic status,[3] their academic standing, and the courses they are taking and have taken in related areas such as the social studies. (Some students may even have been exposed previously to part of the moral education program or to something similar, through the efforts of an enterprising teacher.) While every effort should be made to control those parts of the treatment that are believed to be absolutely essential, that in effect define what the treatment is — e.g., a minimum number of minutes per week spent in discussing moral dilemmas, a minimum number of value sheets distributed to the class each month, a minimum number of hours spent at action-placement sites each week — variation may be permitted and even encouraged in everything else. To quote Cronbach (1978) again, "Planning an evaluative inquiry is [or at least it should be] more like planning a program of investigation than like planning a single experiment.... In principle, anything not pinned down as constant by the definition [of the treatment] ought, in the realization, to be varied over the realistic range."

Thus, as a practical matter, some teachers will do just the minimum and others will do more; some will supplement the program with procedures of their own while other will not. In some schools, the climate will be conducive to a great deal of classroom discussion while in other schools it will not be; and within schools of each kind, and among both treatment and control groups, some teachers will encourage discussion

---

[3]There is evidence (Sharf, 1978b; Lundberg, 1974) that moral status and growth, at least in the Kohlbergian sense, are in part a function of socioeconomic status.

while others will discourage it.[4] These and other variations, when considered in conjunction with the ultimate findings of the evaluation, can help identify what really is essential to it and what is not.

Evaluation designs that have been modified in such ways are generally referred to as "quasi-experiments." There are two basic strategies for quasi-experimental designs, the use of comparison groups and time-series analyses. A comparison group is used in a quasi-experimental design in lieu of a control group when randomized assignment procedures are not used. In the typical case, students in the experimental group (or what in a quasi-experiment should be referred to as the "treatment" group) have elected to enroll in the moral education program rather than take some other course or courses. In this case, the treatment group consists of the volunteers and the comparison group or groups consists of the students in those other courses. If we apply the premeasures and postmeasures to the treatment and comparison groups, outcome measures will potentially be influenced by a variety of extraneous factors. Some of these effects may be directly related to the self-selection process, and others may be attributable to different sources. The task of the evaluator is to devise an appropriate set of strategies to estimate or control for these sources of bias.

In pursuing possible sources of bias introduced by self-selection, the investigator needs to explore a number of different questions concerning the processes by which students came to volunteer. Did a particular clique or friendship network jointly decide to enroll in the program? Did teachers encourage individuals to enroll on the basis of their perception of student needs or their perception of student potential to benefit from the program? If so, what criteria were used in selecting students for encouragement? Did some students not volunteer because they were unaware of the program? If so, what dimensions might underlie their unawareness? Answers to these questions will provide clues for appropriate extraneous and potentially biasing variables.

A simple procedure to identify potentially contaminating or extraneous variables involves comparing the groups' characteristics on a number of dimensions. Candidates variables for this kind of comparative analysis might include sex, race, age, grade-point average, and aptitude or achievement scores. The problem confronting the evaluator here is to select carefully these extraneous variables for group comparisons. In order to do so, the investigator must have an intimate knowledge of both the theoretical foundation underlying the program and the content of program activities. This knowledge should be complemented with in-depth information on psychological, sociological, economic, and political dimensions of the high-school culture. This is the kind of information

---

[4]Flowers (1978) has suggested that group discussions in which teachers participate as equals may enhance moral growth regardless of whether moral dilemmas are the subject matter.

which can only be gathered by immersing oneself in both the program and the social context of the school, the kinds of activities we recommend in an exploratory study.

Frequently, some criteria other than self-selection may be involved in the assignment of students to a moral education program. For example, if more students than the program can accommodate volunteer, they might be assigned on the basis of grade-point average. In this case, we would expect initial differences among the experimental and comparison groups. If grade-point averages and the moral-status measure are related, the evaluator must consider the possibility of so-called "regression effects," which refer to the fact that performance on outcome measures may regress toward the group average over time. Again, a thorough understanding of the theoretical rationale, objectives, and procedures, and an intimate knowledge of the high school are the only bases on which to make decisions concerning appropriate comparison variables.[5]

The second basic strategy employed in quasi-experiments is the time-series design. In this design, periodic measurements are taken before the program begins, during the program, and after the program ends. If the program produces a definite change, the patterns before and after will be markedly different. As depicted in Figure 3.4 the time-series design is partially comparable to an experiment. Measurements taken before can be interpreted as control-group data. However, the possible contaminating effects of historical events or normal maturation cannot be isolated in the time-series design.

This design is substantially strengthened when extended to a combination of comparison group and time series. The resulting format, the multiple-time-series design, is depicted in Figure 3.5. If measures relevant to desired program outcomes are routinely collected on all students at regular intervals during their high-school careers, this design can be very useful as well as relatively inexpensive to implement.

In the figure, the solid line indicates the average scores for all students combined up to the time when the program begins. The dashed line shows the average score increase for students who participate in the program. The dotted line, representing students who have not taken the program, shows that average scores remained the same. Students who completed the program continued to show smaller gains in measurements taken after the program ends, but they are not as large as the increases which resulted during the program.

In our opinion, it is very important for evaluations of moral education programs to be undertaken with the most flexible approach

---

[5]When we have reason to suspect that the treatment and comparison groups differ, we can gain some insight into the effect these differences have on outcome measures by employing an analysis of covariance. See the discussion in Chapter 5 on analysis.

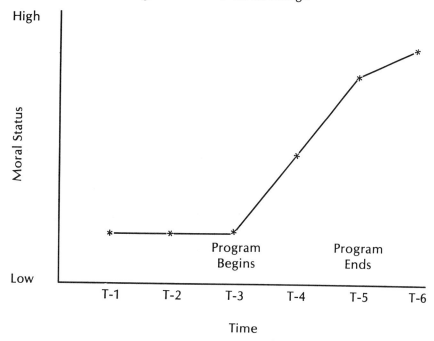

Figure 3.4: Time-Series Design

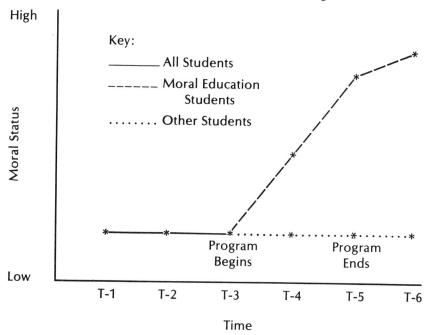

Figure 3.5: Multiple-Time-Series Design

possible. Comparison-group and time-series designs may be used simultaneously, and investigators should not be hesitant to employ various other combinations. Even when the initial design is in place, there is no reason why data cannot be collected during the course of the program to investigate other possible contaminating variables. It is usually not possible to guard against every possible source of bias in a design before the program is undertaken, and the investigator should not hesitate to innovate and make additions to the design. This is referred to as "patching up" the evaluation (Campbell and Stanley, 1966). This flexibility in adapting and patching designs should be extended to include repeating evaluations in successive years of the program's operation. Obviously, the results obtained in one year will influence decisions as to which factors the evaluator might wish to examine in subsequent years.

We want to emphasize that it is unrealistic to expect the evaluation of the outcome of a program to prove definitive after the program's first data year. Evaluation of moral education programs must necessarily employ a longer time perspective, for it is naive to expect conclusive results in a one-year period. The very nature of moral education programs suggests that the effect of such programs may not surface in the short period of one school year. Those programs in which students are enrolled for two or more years will in all probability be able to demonstrate more convincingly the effect of the program. This longer time perspective should broaden the vision and scope of the evaluation providing for different forms of quasi-experimental designs in succeeding years.

Chapter Four

GOALS AND MEASURES IN MORAL EDUCATION PROGRAMS

The conventional wisdom has it that the first step in performing an evaluation must be to state clearly the goals that the program to be evaluated is expected to reach — and in this case, the conventional wisdom is largely correct. It is true that one school of thought holds that evaluations ought to be "goal-free" (Scriven, 1972). What this means is that evaluators should feel free to study whatever happens in connection with a program, whether it has been stated as a goal or not. However, the very purpose of an evaluation is to furnish information about what a program has (or has not) done; and if one has no expectations of what it *might* do, it will be impossible to find out whether the program has done them. Among these expectations are the goals of those involved in the program, and to ignore those goals would be discourteous, not to say perverse, and could well render the evaluation sterile if not stillborn. So, whatever else may be the objects of evaluation, some set of goals will surely be included. Beyond these propositions lie some fairly complicated problems concerning just what the goals of moral education ought to be.

The varieties of goals

The first of these problems is that many different people are involved in an educational program and its evaluation, and they will not all have the same goals. All of the practitioners and consumers that have been mentioned above will probably have ideas about what the aims of moral education ought to be. Furthermore, there may well be differences of opinion within any one of these categories; some parents, for example, will look for one sort of result, while others will look for different ones. Organized groups in the community, or the media, may have still other views. The program's designers will have ideas of their own, and so would an "outside" agency, such as a government department or a foundation which is funding the program. Experienced evaluators will themselves have ideas about what might happen in a moral education program. Both the desire for support of the ultimate results of the evaluation and — as was suggested in Chapter 2 — the very nature of moral education demands that the attitudes of all these groups and individuals be taken into account when the evaluation is being planned. It is quite possible that, when that is done, it will be found that some of the goals are contradictory to others, but that should not be regarded as a problem: the evaluation can nevertheless provide information on the degree to which each of them was realized. Better to retain these different goals than to force a consensus on a goal statement that is so vague that it not only masks the differences but makes impossible the determination of whether the goal was achieved — e.g., the program will "strengthen the moral fiber of students."[1]

What may be a more serious difficulty is that the cost — in money and in the skills and time of people — of studying a vast array of goals may be prohibitive, and then some economically supportable choices will have to be made. In that case, primary attention will presumably have to be given to the goals of those who will pay for the evaluation and those who will be expected to act (or who might be able to prevent action) on the basis of its findings.

A second problem is that, especially in an area such as moral education, it may be a long time before one knows whether the important goals of a program — the main reasons why the program was initiated —have been realized. Furthermore, over a long period of time, there will be many factors which can affect the achievement of the program's goals but which are outside the program's control (e.g., changes in the composition of the student body, in the moral climate of the community, or even in the nature of television programming). For such reasons, the evidence about goal achievement, when it does become available, is often not clearcut. Consequently, some people have urged that a program's goals include some short-term ones; even though they are less important than the long-term ones, they will make possible some "interim signals" about whether the program is moving in the right

---

[1]Note that while multiple and conflicting goals for the program can be tolerated, there would still have to be agreement on the goals of the evaluation if it is to have the kind of support it needs. What we are suggesting is that, where program goals differ, the parties involved be persuaded to agree to disagree, so that the evaluation can go forward.

direction or is accomplishing some desirable things, such as an improvement in reading skills, that are not even pertinent to the main goals (cf. Patton, 1978). There is some merit in that advice. However, it should not be pushed too far, lest the evaluation, and the action which grows out of it, eventually come to be guided by what is easy and convenient rather than by what is important. The plan for evaluating a moral education program should include some long-term and short-term goals.

There is at least one more distinction that should be made. An instructional program typically seeks to bring about change in the students, and it proposes to do so by a specified means or set of methods. The sought-for changes in the students are called "outcome goals," while the means of producing them are called "process goals." It is important that both of these be included in the evaluation plan. Outcome goals will be discussed in greater detail in the next section. What has to be said about process goals, however, is different and briefer, and we shall tend to that now.

The usefulness of an evaluation comes from knowing not merely whether the hoped-for changes took place in the students but also what accounts for the changes (or for their absence), so that the program can be run again if warranted, and can be run better. Unless the processes have been monitored — what teachers actually did in the classroom, for example — there will be no way of explaining the outcomes. In addition, knowledge about what processes were actually used, when juxtaposed to knowledge about outcomes, may suggest conclusions about which processes were essential and which could be dispensed with in the future.[2]

One of the major concerns of process goals is whether the program was in fact operated as it was supposed to be operated. This must not be taken for granted. How much classroom time was really devoted to the discussion of moral problems? Were the meetings of the "just community" held as scheduled, and did the teachers behave as equals? How many times in an average school day did a student hear a clarifying remark from a teacher? How many hours a week did students in an actionist program actually spend at their placement sites?[3] Other process

---

[2]The attribution of a particular outcome to the particular process which "caused" it, however, is by not means a self-evident matter. See the discussion in Chapter 3.

[3]In some cases, moral-education programs seem to have only process goals. Thus, one actionist program stated as its "ultimate" goals: "to provide opportunities for all secondary[-school] students...to participate and interact with persons of different ages and backgrounds, and with different lifestyles; to explore larger sections of economic, political and social life; to engage in responsible work and volunteer activities; to have more active and practical learning; and to make worthwhile contributions to their communities." Lockwood (1978) has commented that "values clarification...may be construed as a relatively clear treatment in search of coherent, measurable outcomes, [while] the moral development approach may be characterized as a relatively coherent, measurable outcome in search of a clear treatment that will promote it."

goals will lead to questions that are not different from those that would be asked about a program in any area. Were readings and other materials available when they were needed? Did the teachers use them as they had expected to (and if not, why not)? Did teachers introduce any techniques of their own that were not contemplated in the program plan? Is there evidence that teachers understood the theoretical bases and the intentions of the program, and that they were convinced of the program's value and of its compatibility with their professional outlook? Were they offered, and did they take advantage of, the opportunities for in-service training that were supposed to be provided? In short, the evaluation must determine just what happens when the program was implemented, or what "the program" actually consisted of. It should be noted that close monitoring of processes is an especially important part of formative evaluation.

Outcome goals

In describing the various types of moral education programs (Chapter 2), we pointed out that they tend to emphasize the learning of skills in the *process* of reasoning about moral problems, rather than the acquisition of specific substantive moral views. This distinction is often alluded to as one between "form" and "content."[4] The preference for goals of form over goals of content has a philosophical justification. The variety and complexity of human interrelationships are so vast, and the conflicts among moral principles so common, that there are very few moral decisions that can be said in advance to be appropriate to a particular situation. (Another way of putting this is to say that it is impossible to specify in advance all the particularities of a situation that would be relevant to a moral decision.) What is indicated, then, is that students should be taught a mode of reasoning which *can* be used in any situation. The preference for form has a tactical appeal as well. Any substantive moral view may encounter opposition from some segment of the community, whereas, as Howard Mehlinger (1978) has asked rhetorically, "Who, after all, can be against thinking?"

Yet, for two reasons, the preference for form over content should not be pressed too far. First, the distinction is harder to sustain than might appear. The forms of moral reasoning are themselves subject to moral judgment; the choice of rationality over tradition, for example, surely has moral implications and can be treated as a moral problem. (People *have* been known to oppose thinking when they feared it might lead to

---

[4]It should not be confused with the distinction between outcome and process goals which we discussed above. There, we were differentiating between the outcomes of a program or changes in students, and the means by which those outcomes were to be produced. Here, we are distinguishing, *within* the outcomes, between those which refer to changes in the *way* students think (form) and those which refer to changes in *what* they think (content).

conclusions they were unwilling to accept.) Thus, form is part of content. Second, there is probably some moral content that virtually everyone would not merely agree on but even insist on, at least as a basis for public instruction and for the conduct of schools as social organizations. Among these elements of content are that, in general, students are expected to be courteous to those with whom they interact, and particularly to refrain from violence or threats of violence. They are also expected to be honest in general and not to cheat in their school work particularly. They should prefer moral choices based on accurate and relevant information over choices based on inaccurate or irrelevant information, choices based on more information over those based on less information, choices based on reason over those based on prejudice (cf. Coombs, 1971). It is difficult to see why these outcomes could not be included among the goals of a moral education program, or indeed how a program can avoid doing so.[5]

Such a position, however, need not and should not preclude instruction in the reasoning that leads to these expectations. In other words, there are at least some instances in which no choice need be made between form and content. An analogy might be drawn with mathematics. Students are expected to believe that the Pythagorean theorem is true, but they are also expected to know how it is proven. Of course, there are more instances of this in the mathematical domain than in the moral, but that is no reason to refrain from using those we have.

We also noted in Chapter 2 that a moral education program has both a cognitive and an affective component; correspondingly, it would need to have both cognitive and affective goals. Among the cognitive outcome goals might be improvements in:

—the ability to perceive the moral aspects of a situation in which a decision has to be made.

—the ability to determine the kinds of knowledge that are relevant to a moral decision.

—the ability to recognize the "parties" (individuals, groups or categories of people, institutions) whose well-being will be affected by the decision.

—knowledge (or ability to acquire the knowledge) about what the needs and wishes of the other parties are, as well as about their moral stances.

—the ability to devise or imagine a wide range of possible actions when faced with a decision situation.

—knowledge (or ability to acquire the knowledge) about the probable effects of one's actions on the well-being of others.

---

[5]Even Kohlberg has used the fact of whether students cheat on a test as evidence of their stage of "moral reasoning" (Kohlberg, 1971).

—understanding of the concepts relevant to moral reasoning (e.g., justice, duty, rights, freedom, responsibility, authority, compassion, equality, integrity).

—ability to articulate one's own and others' moral positions.

—knowledge of the requirements of a rational argument.

—the ability to put all of these together so as to arrive at and defend a moral decision while recognizing the critical points in the argument that could lead others to different decisions (or that might lead one to change one's own decision in the future).

—awareness of the ambiguities in most moral situations and of the reasons for them.

Some of these goals would overlap with those of other portions of an overall educational program — e.g., "knowledge about the needs and wishes of others" and "knowledge about the probable effects of one's actions on the well-being of others" with the social studies, and ability "to perceive the moral aspects of a situation" and "to articulate a moral position" with English — but that is unavoidable and even educationally desirable (although it complicates the task of evaluating the moral education program as distinct from the social-studies or English program).

The emotions are sometimes thought of as the "enemies" of reason and hence of moral rationality. For some emotions, in some circumstances, that is probably true. On the other hand, moral thought and conduct over the long run require the positive support of the emotions.[6] Thus, a moral education program requires affective as well as cognitive outcome goals. Among the possibilities are the cultivation or strengthening of:

—the belief that moral considerations are important in making decisions.

—the desire to take the wishes and needs of others into account when making decisions.

—preferences of the sort mentioned earlier: courtesy over rudeness and indifference, peaceability over violence, honesty over dishonesty, informed reasoning over ignorance and irrationality.

—tolerance for the moral views and decisions of others.[7]

One of the most troublesome and controversial problems in the design and evaluation of moral education programs is whether their

---

[6]Coombs (1971) points out that the cognitive demands of a moral decision are dependent to some extent on the values one attaches to the elements in the situation; to that extent, affect precedes cognition. For some other and especially interesting observations on the relationships between reason and emotion in morality and moral education, see Downey and Kelley (1978), pp. 92-121.

[7]With respect to many of these outcome goals, but conspicuously with respect to this last, there are limits to their applicability, to the range of situations in which we would want to see them displayed. How much tolerance is owed to those whose moral views are threatening or repugnant? Ought one, for example, be tolerant of a group of people who urge genocide?

outcome goals should be stated in terms of mental phenomena — thought, reasoning, judgment — or in terms of overt behavior or action. Favoring the latter position is the contention that it is after all behavior, not thought, which affects other people and is thus the acid test, if not the essence, of morality. It would be difficult to support a program which changed the way students thought but left their actions unaffected — or worse yet, gave them sophisticated rationales for doing whatever self-gratifying things they might want to do.[8] On the other hand, as we have said before, the relationships between thought and action are very complex. The same action can be the result of many different mental states — fear, habit, calculation of gain, or impulse, as well as the desire to contribute to the well-being of others — but only when the action is performed for this last reason would we call it "moral" (Wilson, 1972, p. 18). Thus, the morality of an action depends on the reason why it was done, and if so, it is thought rather than action which defines morality. The apparent conclusion is that an unequivocally moral action is one which contributes to the well-being of others *and* is performed *because* it contributes to the well-being of others. Once more, we see that the goals of a moral education program need to be broadly inclusive.[9]

Up to this point, we have been talking about goals which are "program-free" — i.e., which could be part of any kind of moral education program. In addition to these, however, each type of program, and perhaps even each particular program, will presumably have goals more or less peculiar to it. Thus, a developmental program might seek to raise the moral-judgment level of a specified proportion of students by at least one stage, to prevent fixation at any of the lower stages, and to widen the range of situations to which students apply the highest stage of thought of which they are capable (Rest, 1974a). A values-clarification program's goals might include making students more purposeful, dependable, and consistent in their behavior, and surer of their values (Raths and others, 1966, pp. 10-11; Simon and deSherbinin, 1975), or getting them to make frequent use of values-clarification techniques with each other. An actionist program might seek to cultivate students' willingness to accept responsibility, and both actionist and rationalist programs might aim at enhancing the ability to recognize the need for compromise and to devise mechanisms for compromise.

---

[8]One student (Zalaznick, 1980) who had been a member of a Kohlbergian "just community" for a year reported that some participants displayed attitudes to the effect of "I'm stage 2 and proud of it."

[9]A related issue is whether a moral education program can be deemed successful if the students exposed to it handle in a moral fashion any decisions they find they have to make, or whether it would be expected that students will actively search out opportunities for contributing to the well-being of others. Here again, it would seem to be the sensible course of action to include both kinds of goals.

Whatever the goals of a program may be, it is essential that they be stated with sufficient clarity to allow one to discern whether they are being achieved. Admittedly, and especially in moral education, this is easier to say than do. Goal statements referring to the characteristics of moral thought and behavior tend to be lofty and highly general—and consequently vague. There are no rules that can be laid down for avoiding this, but we have tried to present some good examples in the preceding discussion. "Students should prefer moral choices based on accurate and relevant information" is better than "Students should understand the need for good information," because the former is more precise than the latter and so lends itself more readily to observation. Similarly, "Students show courtesy to each other" is better than "Students relate well to each other," "Students can devise or imagine a wide range of possible actions when faced with a decision situation" is better than "Students can think creatively." A general guideline is that the more specific instances of goal realization can be named, the clearer and more easily observable the goal probably is. These specific instances are sometimes referred to as "objectives," and it is often helpful to accompany a goal statement with a list of objectives, as a step toward rendering the extent of goal-attainment visible in the course of the evaluation.

Finally, an evaluation design must consider the possibility of unintended outcomes. These are obviously not "goals" of a program but they may be just as important as goals. Some of them may be desirable; for example, participation in a just community may raise students' attendance rates, or engagement with materials on a knotty moral problem may improve reading skills. Some of them may not be desirable: tension produced by discussion of difficult moral problems may lower attendance rates, or interest in an action-learning placement may diminish attention to conventional schoolwork. Some of them may even be difficult to anticipate at all. It is here that one may turn for help to a competent evaluation specialist. Such a person will know how to organize data collection so as to enhance the probability that unanticipated events or tendencies will come to attention. This is part of what is meant by goal-free evaluation.

Measuring goal attainment

Once the goals have been formulated, the next task will be to locate or devise ways of knowing whether the goals are being reached. This means, in effect, finding ways of rendering visible the moral status and characteristics of students, so that we can discover whether they are becoming "more moral" or "less moral" or not changing in moral respects. This brings us to one of the most difficult, uniquely difficult, parts of evaluation in the domain of moral education. In the past, research about the morality of children was based on the premises that the nature of moral values and their application to any particular case were self-evident matters; that all the important moral values could be inferred from those held in the areas of sex and aggression; and that adherence to moral values was satisfactorily measured by adherence to the social conventions (see Pittel and Mendelsohn, 1966). Obviously, it is no longer possible to be content with such simplifying premises. We must wrestle anew with the thorny problem: How *does* one measure so elusive a thing as "morality?"

In the discussion which follows, our purpose is to present a broad array of options for dealing with the need to have evidence of what the program is accomplishing. We will concentrate on the more troublesome parts of the measurement problems, leaving aside the more strictly "informational" parts. (Some help with the latter may be found in EPIE Institute, 1976.) Even at that, it will not be possible to discuss in detail every potentially useful instrument and procedure. We will not get into technical issues such as the reliability and validity of various measures; for help with these, it would be well to seek out the advice of a measurement specialist, such as a psychometrician. As in the rest of this handbook, we are trying here only to enlarge readers' awareness and help them get started with the task; we do not pretend to give them everything they need to know.

We will discuss four kinds of measurement devices which might be used in moral education programs:

1. Constructed statements, in which students are presented with a story or question and asked to make a comment or response in their own words, either orally or in writing.

2. Presented statements, in which the students are asked to choose among several alternatives that have already been formulated for them, or to arrange the alternatives in some order or to place some degree of value on each one.

3. On-site observations, in which third persons are present with the students in some relevant situation and are asked to count specified kinds of acts or, later, to rate or describe their behavior.

4. Off-site observations, in which third persons assemble and interpret data derived from the student's actions although the third persons were not present when the actions were performed.

Constructed statements. The great advantage of this kind of measure, most familiar in the form of interviews and essays, is that it allows students to express their own ideas, opinions, and feelings, rather than have to force them into somebody else's mold. The statements thus convey a sense of authenticity; they show what students "really think." This seeming advantage is somewhat offset, however, by the fact that, in order for the students' expressions to be useful in the evaluation, someone must subsequently decide what they meant — i.e., someone must classify the elements of their statements into categories that can be used to summarize the expressions of large numbers of students. Not only does this tend to obscure the original statements (though parts can be retained for use in adding richness, color, and persuasive vividness to the evaluation reports), but it also raises the problem of accuracy of interpretation, and it is a complex, time-consuming, and expensive task. Another problem is that many students have difficulty in expressing their thoughts clearly and coherently. Some students can do so more readily in speaking than they can in writing, but to interview each student individually adds still more to the time and cost required. If students are asked to write their statements, to save the time of interviewing them, there is no opportunity to probe their responses to ensure that the relevant topics are covered. Another cost- and time-saving procedure that can be adopted is to ask students to construct only brief statements — e.,g., to write only one sentence, or even to furnish only the ending to a sentence whose first part is presented to them — but by the same token such statements cannot represent their thoughts as fully as those which are not so restricted. Much of the advantage of the constructed-statements procedure is thereby lost.

In the field of moral education, the constructed-statements device which has been by far the most influential is the Moral Judgment Interview (MJI), the instrument which Kohlberg used in his original research on the moral development of young people. As we have already said, it consists of a set of moral dilemmas, in either written or oral form, each one followed by a series of open-ended questions which respondents are asked to answer in their own words (see p. 17 for an example). Partly because it was such a path-breaking instrument, and partly because Kohlberg and others have published such a wealth of research using it — so that its scale of measurement, the six stages, has become familiar to everyone in the field — it has set the standard for many other measurement efforts. It has been used for evaluation of several moral education programs, though not always successfully. In particular, the scoring of the interviews has proven to be difficult. The scoring system is of course based on Kohlberg's theory; extended special training is required to learn how to use it,[10] and Kohlberg himself has made major changes in it several times. Use of the MJI may entail acceptance of the stage theory of development; at any rate, no one has tried to score the MJI independently of this theory, and it is not at all clear that it could be done.

A constructed-statements instrument that is not derived from the MJI is the Measure of Moral Values (Hogan and Dickstein, 1972).

---

[10]It seems to be a corollary of Kohlberg's theory that not many people can do the scoring. One of the basic axioms of the theory is that people use (i.e., are "at") the highest stage which they are capable of understanding. Since scorers must obviously be able to understand all the statements they might encounter, it appears to follow that they have to be at stage 6 or at least at stage 5 in order to be fully competent.

Respondents are presented with 15 brief statements, such as they might hear in everyday conversation, and are asked to write one-line "reactions" to each. These reactions are scored according to whether they contain or imply one of four "scoring elements": "Concern for the sanctity of the individual, judgments based on the spirit rather than the letter of the law, concern for the welfare of society as a whole, and capacity to see both sides of an issue." This instrument has been used only with college students, though the reading level would certainly be within the capacity of most high-school students. A more serious problem is that it has not had enough use to establish confidence in its characteristics. Also outside the Kohlbergian framework, Hoffman (1970) has given children story beginnings and has asked them to write endings, but scoring of these is no less difficult than in the MJI.

Presented statements. These may take the form of questions with ready-made responses, among which students may designate the one they prefer or the one that corresponds most closely to their views; or of statements with which students are asked to agree or disagree (perhaps to varying degrees, such as "strongly agree" or just plain "agree"), or to which they are asked to give a rating such as "high" or "low" or "important" or "unimportant." Items of this kind can be self-administered and they can be answered rapidly, and they can also be scored rapidly as well as objectively (i.e., there is rarely doubt about which of the responses a student intended to check). But of course they limit students' responses to those which are provided, although in the best instances these responses are derived from interviews with students. Students may and should be permitted to write in their own responses when they do not find one they are willing to accept; but to the extent that they do so the procedure loses its advantages.

Several instruments have been developed using presented statements to measure the moral status of students. The most widely used of these is the Defining Issues Test (Rest, 1974b, 1979, 1980, n.d.). The DIT is based on the theory of cognitive-moral development and so uses six Kohlbergian dilemmas. Following each dilemma are 12 statements, each one designed to represent an issue that would be salient at one or another stage of moral development. Students are asked to rate, on a 5-point scale, how important they think the item should be in determining the actions to be taken by the characters in the dilemma.[11]

---

[11]After rating all items, subjects are asked to indicate the four that they regard as most important in each set; the relationship between the ratings and the rankings is used as a "consistency check," to detect questionnaires on which responses were merely chosen at random. Some of the statements were "written to sound impressive and sophisticated but...don't mean anything" (Rest, 1980); these were included, as they commonly are in instruments of this type, to spot any tendency to assign importance to statements merely because they sound complex rather than because they reflect the subject's views.

In the process of developing the DIT, Rest also wanted to assure himself that it related "to value commitments as well as to purely cognitive capacities" and also to "responses to

Of course, it is also possible to devise one's own instrument, either using presented statements or calling for students to construct statements. This is especially likely to be necessary for programs other than those based on the theory of congnitive-moral development, since these others have not had the advantage of springing from a research instrument; in addition, their designers and advocates have paid much less attention to the development of instruments for measuring outcomes (partly because their outcome goals are less well-defined). The Constitutional Rights Foundation offers evaluation instruments to teachers using its rationalist-program materials, but these are largely tests of knowledge about the legal system, with a few items concerning attitudes toward law-enforcement agencies and agents. Publishers of social-studies textbooks also routinely provide evaluation instruments, but — even when moral issues are dealt with in the text — these instruments, too, are mostly factual (EPIE Institute, 1976); moreover, they are intended for evaluation of student performance rather than of program effectiveness.

Those who set out to devise their own instruments should be warned: It is a complex and technically demanding task, which can consume a substantial part of a program's resources. The process has to be started very early in the development of the program itself, even before the program is launched, so that there will be time to try out items and the administration and scoring of instruments and make the needed revisions and still have an instrument ready for use as a baseline measure or pretest. There are many pitfalls along the way; to name but one, it is easy for an instrument intended to measure moral status to become, in effect, without anyone's realizing it, a measure of students' general academic (especially verbal) aptitude, or of their ability and willingness to say what pleases the teacher, or even of their socioeconomic status. Instrument development is another point at which the advice of a specialist could be valuable.

Devising one's own instrument does have one not inconsiderable advantage: The items can be fashioned to reflect the goals of the particular program being evaluated. The items need not all ask for outright moral decisions or the reasons for them; such items would probably be the most difficult to invent and to score. But if one of the program's goals is to improve students' ability to perceive the moral aspects of a situation,

---

actual, current value controversies." For this purpose, he devised a measure of attitudes toward "law and order," in which subjects were asked to indicate their degree of agreement with statements about such issues as treatment of criminals, wire tapping, civil disobedience, and youth protest; and another measure of "libertarian democracy," which sought to ascertain the extent to which subjects would "support...civil liberties under favorable circumstances." The DIT score was indeed highly correlated with both these measures (specifically, -.60 with the former and .63 with the latter) which perhaps does establish the "relevance" of the DIT but which also strengthens the suspicion that cognitive-moral development may have important ideological associations, rather than being "content-free." (See Rest, 1974, pp. 5-7 — 5-9.)

they could be presented with the description of a situation (contrived or drawn from recent events) and be asked to list the persons or groups whose well-being is involved. For other goals, they could be asked what the needs and wishes of other parties might be (and to make the distinction between needs and wishes), and/or how to obtain that information; or they could be asked to list as many courses of action as possible that could be taken by the persons in the situation. Responses could be scored for relevance and reasonableness (if the instrument used presented statements, the responses would include some that were relevant and reasonable and some that were not) and the number of relevant and reasonable ones could then be counted.

Another "non-standardized" form of measurement, relying upon constructed rather than presented statements, is to request students to keep diaries or journals in which they recount and reflect upon moral problems they have encountered. Such accounts can be especially useful in actionist programs, where an essential part of the program is to put students into situations where they must deal with or at least observe moral problems of "real life." Without an opportunity to mull over these problems —and we pointed out earlier that such an opportunity is not always available in the classroom — much of the value of the "real life" exposure may be lost. But even in programs other than actionist, the stimulus to spend additional time thinking about the moral implications of everyday events can be valuable. However, if students are asked to keep journals which are to be included in the measurement efforts of the evaluation, some way will have to be found to deal with the problem of privacy and/or of dissimulation by students in order to protect their privacy (although experience with journals has shown that students can be surprisingly, even embarrassingly, frank). Furthermore, very difficult decisions will have to be made about how to use the journal content for purposes of observing goal attainment; "scoring" or other use of the content runs into the same kinds of difficulties as scoring the MJI responses, exacerbated by the fact that the journals of different students will have little or no common content. The importance of clearly stated goals will become fully apparent when these decision have to be made.

On-site observations. The procedures we have been discussing so far all rely in one way or another on the verbal outputs of students. But the controversy over whether moral-education goals should be stated in terms of mental phenomena or behavior has an analogy in measurement: Should the attainment of moral-education goals be measured by verbal outputs, or by actions? The issue cannot be resolved by saying that mental states should be observed via verbalizations and behavioral tendencies via actions. Words can be chosen to conceal thought as well as to reveal it, to impress a reader or listener as well as to express oneself. Although there is evidence that the MJI and the DIT cannot easily be "faked upward," the possibility cannot be lightly dismissed even for these instruments. To many people, actions are more "conclusive" evidence even of intentions and desires than words are. On the other hand, as we have pointed out above, motives are a necessary part of the moral interpretation of any action, and yet an action is usually compatible with a variety of motives, so inferring thought from action may not be easy, either. Some goals are very difficult to observe through actions — e.g., the acquisition of morally relevant knowledge — and some are intrinsically verbal — e.g., the ability to articulate a moral position. Indeed, when such verbalizations occur in "real" situations (rather than in interviews or essays), they may be construed as the very actions to be observed. We repeat what is by now a familiar refrain: It would be well for an evaluation of a moral education program to include both verbal and action measures.

Decisions will have to be made about what kinds of actions (or verbalizations) are to be observed, by whom, and where. There are few satisfactory precedents to go by here. Much of the research on children's moral behavior has used, as the indicator, whether they cheat on a test when presented with the opportunity to do so in a contrived situation, but it is doubtful that an evaluation in a naturalistic setting could follow that procedure. However, it would be possible to observe the frequency of acts of courtesy and generosity, of references to the needs and wishes of other people and of efforts to learn about those needs and wishes, of the use of rational argument in moral discourse and — even more telling if it occurs — the frequency of yielding to the rational argument of another. An attempt should be made to identify at least one action for each program goal that could be observed in a natural setting. Less focused observations, leading to general descriptions of what transpired, can also be put to use in the same way — and with the same limitations — as constructed statements. Brickell (1976) has made the interesting suggestion that unfocused observation can also be the source of presented statements for subsequent incorporation into evaluation instruments, instead of having to infer them hypothetically from program goals.

Classroom teachers would of course be one logical choice of observers; they are continuously evaluating students' behavior in any event. But they may not have the time or concentration for making precise counts. A sympathetic colleague (preferably not a control-group teacher, however) or even a parent might perform this function, and might be able to give feedback on the teacher's own behavior as well (is it consistent with the moral principles being taught?). In many cases, the most appropriate observer by virtue of objectivity and training as well as available time will be a person engaged specifically for the evaluation. In each of these cases, some means will have to be provided to the observers for recording their observations systematically in a way that will yield information comparable across the different settings in which the observations are made. Alternatively, observers could be asked to make ratings of student behavior, growing out of their general knowledge of the students, rather than to make precise counts of their actions. The originators of values clarification in particular recommend the use of teachers' ratings for evaluation purposes (Raths and others, 1966, pp. 177 ff.). Even students can make useful observations, not on the behavior of specific other students (that would raise obvious ethical objections) but on the frequency with which they encounter certain kinds of actions among their classmates generally.

As the preceding comments suggest, the classroom is an obvious place in which to make the observations, especially the classroom sessions of the treatment and control groups, because then the relevant students are all together and can be observed more efficiently. But there are other possibilities: Teachers of other classes in which treatment or control students are enrolled can also be asked to make observations or ratings, and parents can do the same at home. In actionist programs, placement supervisors would be important observers of student behavior.

Off-site observations. The preceding discussion may sound as if we are suggesting that evaluations be done by "spying" upon students. It is not intended that way. All observation should be done openly, with the students being aware that an observer is present. Some would even take the position that, if students' actions are to be observed, the forms and purposes of observation be explained to them at the outset. This carries the serious risk, however, that it will alter the very actions that were to be observed. Students conscious of being "on display" may very well act differently than they would otherwise. The mere presence of an observer may have some of that effect even without lengthy explanation.

The risk need not be exaggerated. Skilled observers can make themselves inconspicuous; after they have been present on a few occasions students will often forget about them. If the observers are teachers or parents, they are merely part of a kind of situation in which morally relevant actions are frequently performed; if students "alter" their behavior in the presence of these adults, it may be presumed that they would similarly alter their behavior in the presence of other adults — i.e., that the "altered" behavior is their real behavior in certain situations.

Nevertheless, it cannot be denied that, to the potential audience of an evaluation, some suspicion would attach to behavioral data about students derived from situations in which students knew they were being observed for their moral behavior. To deal with similar conditions in other kinds of research and evaluation, the concept of "unobtrusive measures" has been put forth (Webb and others, 1966). The idea behind these measures is that actions often leave "traces" of one sort or another — physical traces or paper traces (records). Thus, students' actions should be observed not by having an observer present during the actions but by classifying and counting the traces that the actions left behind. So, for example, the effectiveness of a moral education program might be measured by a reduction in the number of books overdue at the school library, or in the number of lockers broken into or other instances of vandalism, or by an increase in the amount of money or time contributed by students to charitable or "public-service" causes.

Unobtrusive measures are an appealing notion, but they do have their drawbacks. It is not as easy as it might seem to think of traces that can be identified as the marks of "moral" or "immoral" actions without too much equivocation — bearing in mind especially what we said earlier about the importance of the motive of an act in interpreting its moral significance. Actions and their traces are affected by many forces irrelevant to a moral education program; for example, new locks are installed on the lockers, or a change in transportation schedules makes it harder for students to get to the day-care center where they had been doing volunteer work after school. Some goals, as we said earlier, cannot be observed through actions at all, and so neither can they be observed through the traces of actions. When the fact that unobtrusive measures are being used becomes known to the students (as sooner or later it surely will), they lose their unobtrusive character — i.e., students may take that use into account when acting. Still, evaluators of moral education programs would be well-advised to include some unobtrusive measures in their plans. Data for them are relatively inexpensive to collect, and they have a "real-life" quality about them that can be quite persuasive.

Conclusions

It should be abundantly clear by now that the evaluation of a program in moral education demands multiple measures of effectiveness. The program will probably have a large number of goals, both process and outcome, and there will be interest as well in processes and outcomes that have not been expressed as goals and may even be unwanted. Obviously, no one measure is capable of encompassing all of this. Even for any single goal, there is no single method of measuring its attainment that commands or deserves universal acceptance. Each procedure yields a different sort of information, subject to its own ambiguities. If too much reliance is placed on a small number of measures, there is the danger that something will go awry and render the data meaningless. Given the complexities and subtleties of moral education, small amounts of data from each of many different methods will be a more reliable basis for judgment, and a more convincing basis for action, than a large amount collected by one or a few procedures. If all the bits of data point in the same direction, it is probably safe to infer that that has been the direction of the program; if they point in different directions, then it would have to be said that the program has evidently had mixed effects, and knowing that is better than having knowledge, however firm, about only one of these effects. If this whole chapter were to be reduced to a single word, the word would be: *diversify!*

Chapter Five

ANALYZING AND REPORTING

Reliability and validity

It is rare in social-science research and evaluation that we are able to measure directly the phenomena in which we are interested. Instead, what we observe are "indicators" of these phenomena. This naturally raises questions about the logical and psychological connection of the indicators with the phenomena they are supposed to measure. The two major questions are those concerning reliability and validity.

The reliability of a measure is the extent to which it produces (or would produce) consistent results in repeated applications. Whether the measure is a field observation, responses to an interview, or a selection from among several presented answers, its reliability is the probability of obtaining the same result in the same circumstances. Hence, reliability is a statement of the stability or dependability of a measurement.

Suchman (1967) indentified five types of reliability:

(1) subject reliability, which refers to variations in the subject such as motivation or fatigue that may produce unsystematic variations in responses;

(2) observer reliability, referring to variations in and among observers that influence their observations and interpretations;

(3) situational reliability, or variations in the measurement situation that may produce aberrations in outcomes;

(4) instrument reliability, having to do with the characteristics of the measurement itself; and

(5) processing reliability, referring to the possibility of unsystematic errors occurring in the coding or processing of data.

The optimal strategy for insuring high reliability is careful monitoring of those factors which may cause errors in the measurement. A closely monitored evaluation project is one of the best protections against unreliability. All individuals involved in any form of data collection must be throroughly trained to insure that they are following appropriate and comparable procedures. Furthermore, checkpoints should be established to verify that data are being collected and processed without introducing errors into measurements. And finally, some type of repeated measure should be taken and systematic comparisons made.

There are two basic strategies for repeated measures. One is to have several different individuals execute the same measurement process, be it observation, interview, questionnaire, coding, or test administration. The results are then compared among the different measurements. A second procedure is to divide the measurement instruments into two parts. Of course, this is most easily done with paper-and-pencil tests. If the test itself is internally consistent, then scores on each part should be similar. It is impossible to specify an absolute standard for agreement on these types of comparisons. As a rule of thumb, most investigators feel that congruence of 80 percent or greater is acceptable in comparing multiple measures or split-half tests. However, the evaluator must apply individual judgment in determining what is an acceptable level of reliability.

Validity, on the other hand, refers to the degree to which a measure is indeed an indicator of the phenomenon it was supposed to measure —e.g., a goal or objective of the program. Validity and reliability are, of course, related. A measure cannot be valid unless it is also reliable. However, it is quite possible to have a measure which has very high reliability but no validity. Since we are encouraging the use of multiple measures of program outcome, the question of the validity of measures should also be explored in all data analyses.

We frequently distinguish between three types of validity: face, predictive, and construct. Face validity refers to the extent to which the relevance of a measure to a goal is obvious. For example, a simple frequency count of the number of times a student engages in behavior to help others has a definite face validity with respect to the goal of considering the needs or wishes of others. Predictive validity refers to the extent to which a measure is an accurate indicator of other characteristics or especially of future behaviors. Construct validity has to do with the extent to which a measure provides an adequate basis for inferring the degree to which an individual possesses a characteristic which we assume to be reflected in the measurement process. Construct validity is relevant when a characteristic is not something which can be pointed to or identified with a specific behavior but is an abstraction or a construct.

Social scientists tend to agree that the process of determining validity, or "validation," is enhanced by evidence that different measures yield similar results. To secure such evidence, we must measure the construct in question by several different methods. Therefore, the data analysis employed in the evaluation of moral education programs should examine the degree of relationship among the various multiple measures of program goals and objectives. There are a variety of techniques available for this purpose. Cross tabulation is one method which is easily accomplished and understood, and evaluators would be well advised to use it, whatever other techniques they may also use.

Significance of differences

Social scientists have been most adept at producing a wide variety of data analysis procedures, including techniques for comparing group averages and identifying sources of variation. A great deal of attention has been devoted in the literature to specifying the conditions that should guide selection of a technique for data analysis. However, we believe that it is not a wise investment of time or resources on the part of those evaluating moral education programs to devote a great deal of time to selecting the most appropriate data-analysis technique. When a program produces an important outcome, it is usually apparent no matter which data analysis technique is employed. For this reason, we encourage the use of comparisons of group proportions or means in most evaluation designs. Perhaps a so-called "analysis of variance" might be helpful in cases of more elaborate quasi-experimental designs employing multiple experimental and control groups. However, in most instances a simple comparison of means probably will be adequate.

The problem remains of how to determine whether a difference of means between an experimental and a comparison group is sufficiently large to warrant consideration in policy decisions concerning the future of the program. The standard procedure in most social-science research is to employ a test of significance. In the case of comparisons of means, this is usually a t test. This test yields a statistic which can be related to a theoretical probability distribution of the difference between means, permitting one to estimate how frequently differences of the obtained magnitude or greater would occur if the evaluation were repeated many times. This kind of statement would give some confidence in the stability of the obtained difference in program outcomes for the two groups. A complete treatment of the appropriateness of using a t test in evaluations of moral education programs is beyond the scope of this handbook.

However, it is important that we point out one distinction which is commonly misunderstood among evaluators. In much social-science research, tests of significance are used to generalize the results of an analysis of data collected from a sample which has been randomly selected to represent a larger population. Tests of significance in these instances make estimates of the probability that the results found in the sample are accurate descriptions of the larger population. This use of tests of significance in evaluation of moral education programs will in almost all cases be inappropriate, for the students in either experimental or comparison groups will probably not be randomly selected from any larger population. Therefore, generalizations to larger populations in these evaluations will not be appropriate.

Unfortunately, tests of significance are also commonly used to determine whether obtained results have substantive or practical significance. We encourage evaluators not to use tests of significance in this fashion. It is more important to pay attention to the magnitude of the differences in means relative to what one expects to accomplish. For example, if the outcome measure is a student's score on the Kohlberg moral-development scale, which ranges from 1 to 6, a difference of one point is substantively quite important. Whether it is *statistically* significant is much less relevant, particularly for policy considerations. If, however, a test of factual knowledge on the legal-justice system, with scores varying from 1 to 100, is used as an outcome measure, a difference in means of 1 has very little policy relevance, even though under certain conditions, such as when there are large experimental or control groups, it could be statistically significant.

Some cautions

There are several pitfalls which are common in the conduct of evaluations, and we would like to point them out in the hope of helping readers avoid them. Of course, it is impossible to provide any guarantee of the success of an evaluation effort. However, we hope that these warnings will improve the judgment of those involved in the evaluation, for good judgment is an indispensable condition for success.

The Hawthorne effect. In any kind of new program, the participants may behave differently solely because they are subjects in a research activity. This effect was first detected in the now classic studies of employees of the Hawthorne plant of the Western Electric Corporation. Conducted over several years during the 1930s, the Western Electric studies examined levels of worker productivity under a variety of different conditions. The investigators noticed that productivity improved continuously, whether working conditions were made better or worse or were even returned to the way they had been at the start. The investigators concluded that this resulted primarily from the fact that the workers were responding positively to the personal attention they were receiving from the investigators themselves. Their positive feelings caused productivity to rise continuously, regardless of the nature of the experimental conditions (Roethlisberger and Dickson, 1939).

66

It should be pointed out that recently some doubt has been cast upon the accuracy of the data analyses in the original Western Electric studies. It may be that productivity did not uniformly increase under all experimental conditions. Nevertheless, the phenomenon has been demonstrated in other settings, and the name of the "Hawthorne effect" has become firmly entrenched to refer to the possibility that outcome measures may be contaminated by the response of participants to the novelty and excitement of a new program, regardless of substance.

A new moral education program will very likely be the object of attention of not only the teaching staff, but of evaluators, administrators, and perhaps visitors from outside the school as well. All this attention may produce positive feelings on the part of the students. It may also be the case that students in comparison groups may feel excluded from the excitement and attention surrounding the new program. Hence, a feeling of alienation may develop among students in the comparison groups, particularly among students who had volunteered for the experimental group but were turned away because of insufficient openings.

One way of determining the magnitude of the Hawthorne effect is to offer a new program *without* a moral education component to at least one group of comparison students. Any change that this group shows in moral status can then be "subtracted" from the gain shown by students in the treatment group, on the assumption that the gain was partly due to program novelty. However, this is not always possible. Short of that, interviewing of students in experimental and comparison groups is the best strategy to uncover the possible existence of a Hawthorne effect. The investigator should be careful not to suggest the idea of Hawthorne effect to the students by the way in which the questions are phrased.

The Pygmalion effect. Another possible source of bias that may influence outcome measures in evaluation research is known as the "Pygmalion effect," so named by Rosenthal (1968) following a series of experiments he conducted in elementary schools. Rosenthal administered standard intelligence tests to students in several classes at the beginning of a school year. Half of the classes were "experimental" groups, in which teachers were given inflated reports of the results of the tests. Teachers of the students in the control groups were given the correct test results. At the end of the school year, Rosenthal again administered standardized tests to the students. He found that students in the experimental classes showed greater gains in their scores, and he contended that this was because the teachers had higher expectations for them, and these expectations resulted in harder work on the part of the students. As with the Hawthorne effect, replications and reanalyses of the original data have cast some doubt on the accuracy of the Rosenthal experiment, but the name nevertheless has stuck, to refer to a phenomenon widely believed to exist.

Attention to the possibility of a Pygmalion effect will be particularly appropriate in moral education program evaluations where students have volunteered to participate in the program. Self-selection may well be a reflection of their greater interest or perhaps heightened sensitivity to the objectives of such programs. If this is perceived by both students and faculty, it can raise teacher expectations concerning student performance. On the other hand, there could be a potential negative Pygmalion effect if students are assigned to the program on the basis of their perceived need for such instruction on the part of faculty or guidance counselors. Here the students might resent being labeled as individuals who "need" moral education and resist teacher efforts to improve their performance.

Again, we recommend that probing, unstructured inverviews be conducted with both students and faculty to determine the extent to which there are preexisting expectations concerning student achievement of the objectives of the program. An interpretation of the results of the evaluation with a view toward future policy formulation should be appropriately modified if there is any evidence to suggest a Pygmalion effect from the interview data.

The difference between impact and coverage. Rossi (1979) has pointed out the need for distinguishing between "impact" and "coverage" in interpreting the results of an evaluation. Results that show that a program made a big difference — i.e., had a substantial *impact* — sometimes lead to the inference that the program can readily produce similar results in other settings — i.e., has broad coverage. It is easy to lose sight of the fact that participants in the program may not at all be representative of the larger group of students either in that school or in others. It is quite possible that the impact could be limited to students of a particular sex, educational level, social class, or personality type. Analyzing the data separately for students of different kinds can help reveal these differences, but the number of distinctions that it is reasonable to make among students is often sharply limited by the small number of participants in the program as a whole. In any event, one should be wary of drawing generalizations about the program's effectiveness for different kinds of students, or for students in school settings and communities unlike those in which it has been evaluated.

The problem of enthusiasm. An evaluator can expect to encounter an inordinate degree of enthusiasm and optimism about the outcomes of a program on the part of those who instituted it. Typically, they will expect outcome measures to show large differences and to provide strong confirmation of the rightness of their decision to undertake the program. But dramatic results are rare in an evaluation, and in the evaluation of a moral education program will be especially rare because of the elusive nature of the goals (and, if our previous advice has been followed, because of the many different sorts of observations that have been made). It behooves the evaluator, then, to try to develop more realistic expectations for the outcomes and their measurement.

The importance of time. Closely related to the problem of enthusiasm is that of time. Educational programs can rarely be expected to show noticeable effects in less than a year. Programs of moral education will almost certainly take even longer, because moral perspective is a deep-lying and slowly changing part of the personality. It is well to plan for a moral education program and its evaluation to be in operation for two or three years or more — although, as we shall point out shortly, that certainly does not mean that no reports about the program should be made before then.

Time is important in an evaluation in another respect as well. A program's ramifications are not known fully or clearly in advance, and again this is apt to be even more true of moral education programs than of others. Consequently, those involved in the evaluation need to have time for reflection, for exchanging ideas with each other and with the participants, for making new observation plans when the circumstances warrant. If the schedule for the evaluation is too tight, if the evaluation team is constantly being pressed to meet deadlines and get on with the next planned steps, many valuable opportunities will be missed.

The protection of privacy. It is now an accepted canon of all research and evaluation that the investigator has an obligation to protect the privacy of subjects. This requirement is particularly important in the case of evaluation in moral education programs because of the delicacy of the issues involved. In the course of the evaluation, a great deal of sensitive information will be collected about the attitudes and behavior of students and teachers, information of a kind not typically exposed in other high-school instruction. While the data must of course be reported accurately, it is incumbent upon the evaluator to take steps to ensure that no information will be released that can be identified with a particular individual. Students and teachers should be fully informed, before the evaluation begins, of its purposes and of the plans for collection, analysis, and reporting of data, and they must be assured that the information they divulge, voluntarily or "involuntarily" (e.g., during classroom observations), will not be transmitted to others in association with their name or wrongfully used in any way. In some circumstances, it would be wise, and may be legally necessary, to obtain written consent statements from all participants.

Reporting the findings

A common criticism of evaluation reports is that they are received too late to be of any use. Decisions about the future of a program often have to be made before the final measurements have been made, the data processed, and the results written up. For an evaluation to be most helpful, then, interim reports about it should be made at frequent intervals. These reports may be written or oral. Indeed, the chief evaluator would be well advised to keep an up-to-date report in mind at all times, ready for delivery on short notice. Not only will these steps enhance the likelihood that the evaluation will be used by decision makers; they will also make it more useful to teachers and others who are charged with the day-to-day implementation of the program, because frequent reports —in the nature of formative evaluation — will help them improve the program as they go along. Frequent reports will also help retain support for the continued conduct of the evaluation. And not least important, interim reports will often elicit reactions and interpretations which will suggest improvements in the evaluation itself — a kind of formative evaluation of the evaluation.

All reports, written or oral, interim or final, must of course be made in a form which is designed to meet the needs of the particular audience. What is sufficient for the local press might not be detailed enough for the teachers; what school-board members are concerned about might not be what students are concerned about. Some audiences may be able to understand technical points and others may not. However, for virtually all audiences, liberal use of anecdotal materials — without, it must be emphasized, identifying by name or description any of the persons involved — makes a report interesting, "alive," and convincing.

Postscript

It has not been our purpose in this handbook to make recommendations on whether a school should or should not have a program in moral education. However, in the course of our work, we have become aware of some of the considerations which bear on that decision, and it may be helpful to present a brief discussion of them. We have placed the discussion here — rather than earlier in the handbook, where it might seem logically to belong — because some of what we want to say requires an understanding of matters treated at various points in the handbook.

In one sense, the decision about whether to have a program in moral education does not have to be made. In every school, students are learning about morality every day — learning from the rules the school has (including those it has but does not enforce), from the ways in which teachers deal with them, from the kinds of behavior and the kinds of treatment of each other that the school tolerates, from the expectations of their behavior on the part of all with whom they interact. In other words, the school *has* a moral education program, in the sense of a set of activities from which students make inferences about proper moral decisions. The real issue is whether a school will allow its moral education program to continue to be entirely implicit and uncontrolled, or whether it will also seek to present an organized, coherent, and purposeful set of learning activities.

Probably the most common argument made against offering an explicit program in moral education is that instruction in morality is the province of the home and the church, not the school. This argument cannot stand up for very long. It is generally recognized by now that effective education for the young is a responsibility shared by all adults and their institutions. Home and church can no more teach morality by themselves than the school can expect students to learn to read without the support of the home. In any event, the school inevitably has rules by which it operates, and it is hard to see how it can decline to defend and justify those rules openly. Can a school reasonably refuse to say why it prefers honesty to cheating, knowledge to ignorance, reason to prejudice, decorum to a war of all against all? And if it is willing to state those reasons openly, why can't those reasons, and the reasoning process in which they are used to form conclusions, be a subject of instruction?

In the last analysis, perhaps the only defensible reason for not offering an explicit program in moral education is a practical one. A school is expected to do a great many things, and it has only limited resources with which to do them. If there is no great demand in the community for a moral education program, it might seem willful to insist upon installing one. Not only might there be a lack of demand: It is quite conceivable that an explicit moral education program would rouse the ire of important segments of the community and make all the rest of the school's work that much more difficult. However, this ought not be taken for granted. In most of the communities we visited, the program had strong community support, built on careful and honest communications about it and later on the enthusiasm of the student and teacher participants. Administrators or school-board members who feel that a moral education program should be offered, or who are being urged to offer one by teachers or parents, ought to explore community sentiment about it before deciding that it wouldn't be worth the trouble. The dedication and responsibility shown by such an exploration might actually improve public attitudes toward the school or school system as a whole.

If the decision is made to go ahead, the question will have to be faced of which type of program to offer, and which particular program within the type. It is difficult to offer advice about this. Very little can be said confidently about the strategies that are most effective in the area of moral education. (That, of course, is one reason why more efforts at evaluation of programs are needed.) Even the advocates of one or another type of program often display a good deal of modesty when it comes to discussing the evidence for their preference (Hill and others, 1977; Mosher, 1980; Raths and others, 1966; Scharf, 1978a). There is probably more evidence for Kohlbergian programs than for any other, but that may be only because they were developed by a researcher and have goals that it is relatively easy to make observable. Even within Kohlbergian programs, it is far from clear whether whatever effects they produce — and those are not unequivocal — are the result of discussions of the Kohlberg dilemmas, discussions of dilemmas generally, discussions of moral issues whether in the form of dilemmas or not, or discussion of serious issues with teachers participating as equals; or perhaps they are simply the result of membership in a "just community." The particular hierarchy of values that is intrinsic to Kohlbergian theory, with justice at its apex, is not acceptable to all, and it may conceal a set of values that would be rejected if it were made explicit (Bennett and Delattre, 1978). Nor has Kohlberg made a convincing case that the sequence of stages is psychologically "natural" or that it is philosophically logical, much less that the psychological naturalness is a product of the philosophical logic as he claims (Hall and Davis, 1975). In short, it may well be that the dominance of Kohlbergian programs is at least premature.

In the absence of clearcut evidence favoring one type of program or another, other criteria will have to be used in choosing among them. Perhaps the most important of them would be the attitude of the instructional staff, for if the teachers are not convinced that a program is worthwhile, it is not likely to be effective whatever else may be true about it. This may in turn require that the teachers be given an opportunity — e.g., in an in-service training experience — to learn about the problems in the field and the kinds of programs that are available. Having had a course or workshop, a group of teachers may then wish to create their own hybrid program or to invent one de novo, and perhaps they will come up with something quite promising. It would be particularly auspicious for the success of a program if the initiative for introducing it came from the teachers in the first place.

Another important consideration, as we have already suggested, would be the community attitude. Indeed, perhaps an early step would be the establishment of a teacher-parent committee to consider the possibilities and make recommendations. Such a committee, with the advice of the school administration and in consultation with the school board, would presumably want to take into account the goals of the program, the nature of its moral principles, and its possible unintended outcomes, and also the cost and availability of materials or other requirements (such as transportation, in an actionist program, or the cooperation of lawyers and police officers, in a rationalist program); the course-load and scheduling implications; the availability of local experts for technical consultation and further in-service training; the administrative location of the program, and whether it should be a single course, a combination of courses, or a schoolwide activity; and, of course, what the evaluation strategies should be.

The committee members should be aware, and they should make others aware, that, whatever the type of program and whatever its position in the curriculum, it will have implications for the organization, structure, and climate of the entire school. One cannot keep the moral issues raised in the classroom separate from the moral issues encountered in the everyday life of the school. On this point, Wilson Riles (1975) has given us a sober warning:

> We cannot expect a student to function as a responsible...citizen at age 18 when his sole knowledge of rights, responsibilities, freedom, justice, and brotherhood has come from negative experiences — from punishment for breaking rules he had no voice in making, from school courses and future occupations chosen for him, from uneven justice for antisocial behavior, from teachers' or administrators' ridicule of individuals, and from too frequent evidence that "good guys finish last."

Appendix A

PROTOTYPES OF MORAL EDUCATION

This appendix contains brief descriptions of prototypes of four moral and civic education programs. Our purposes in presenting the descriptions are twofold. First, we wish to provide readers with additional, concrete examples of program characteristics in the categories of rationalist, actionist, values-clarification, and moral-development education programs. The various features described in these hypothetical examples are drawn from fieldwork conducted during the course of this project, but there is no direct correspondence between the descriptions presented below and any one of the sites visited. Rather, the prototypes draw upon the materials collected during the fieldwork in various combinations. School-board members, administrators, faculty, students, and parents should find it useful to learn how these programs might be initiated and organized, and how they might be currently operating in their school and community settings. Those who are considering the initiation of such programs should find it particularly helpful to learn more of the details of the activities, successes, and evaluation problems that might be encountered.

Second, readers who are already familiar with one or more of these programs will find examples of "real-life facts" encountered during the course of our fieldwork. These data will provide a basis for assessing the accuracy of our observations and the legitimacy of our recommendations concerning evaluation activities.

The Developmental Program at Exurbia High School

The setting. Exurbia is a small, affluent commuter town of approximately 25,000 residents situated 50 miles from a midwestern metropolitan complex. Its residents are mainly upper-class families with a median income of $22,000 per year. There is a small but also affluent minority population. Although the size of Exurbia has remained constant over the past ten years, there is a substantial turnover in population as top-level executives of national and multinational corporations are relocated to and from the various corporate units. Exurbia's residents are more affluent, live in larger homes, and commute greater distances than those of most average suburban communities.

As is true in many midwestern cities, a small percentage of children enroll in private schools, but most attend the local public schools, and as a result there is a great deal of interest and involvement in school activities. Exurbia is politically conservative; most residents are registered Republicans. High local property taxes provide the base for educational facilities and programs.

In 1970, the Exurbia School District drew up a formal set of goals, Needs of Youth, which serves as the framework for curricular offerings in the two elementary schools, the middle school, and the high school. The overall goals, developed by committees of teachers, have been relatively stable, but specific course content is constantly revised. The goals of individual courses are specified in course study plans, which describe student and teacher activities and curriculum materials and are submitted annually to the district office for review.

Exurbia High School. Exurbia High serves 1,750 students in grades 10-12. Eighty-five percent of the students attend a two- or four-year college immediately after graduation. The physical plant consists of nine single-story buildings distributed around two quads. The school has a large auditorium and completely equipped field house, as well as extensive outdoor athletic facilities. Construction began this year on a new, ten-million-dollar addition to the high school. Exurbia High offers a wide variety of academic courses, athletic activities, and extracurricular activities.

There are 66 full-time-equivalent faculty at Exurbia High School. During the next three years, 11 older faculty are expected to retire, but they will not necessarily be replaced by younger teachers. Attrition will absorb some of these reductions, and replacement of the retiring teachers is likely to be accomplished through transfers from cooperating neighboring districts rather than the hiring of younger staff. Exurbia High School is considered a desirable school in which to teach by most of its faculty; indeed, several of the current staff are Exurbia graduates. A large guidance department with five full-time counselors provides services in the following areas: college consultation, work experience, individual diagnostic and adjustment problems, and social-work liaison with community agencies.

Exurbia High has a well-established tracking system. The students are distributed into tracks on the basis of their scores on standardized achievement tests administered in the middle school. Four tracks are used in English, mathematics, and social-studies courses; all science and elective courses are unleveled. Because of recent changes in the achievement tests used in the middle school, there is some difficulty in appropriate placements, and supplementary testing is administered at the beginning of the tenth grade to correct any problems. Reassignment of students in succeeding years is implemented by counselors' recommendations on the basis of student performance and faculty evaluations. A student's placement in the three subject tracks is frequently at different levels in the different courses. More than half of the Exurbia High School student body is at the college preparatory track, Level 4, with an average of 52 percent of the students assigned; students wishing to enter the state university are required to complete a minimum number of level 4 course requirements. In addition to the Civic Education Developmental Program (CEDP), Exurbia High has several other special programs, such as the "Opportunity Class" designed for students with behavior problems, small classes for the educationally handicapped, and remedial English and mathematics programs funded by Title I, ESEA. In addition, there is a cross-district Regional Occupation Center which administers a vocational-education program across several districts and in which a small number of Exurbia High students participate.

The Program. The Civic Education Developmental Program at Exurbia High School is a local adaptation of the civic education program developed at Carnegie-Mellon University, which, in turn, is related to the work of the Moral Education Center at Harvard University. The program at Exurbia offers a two-year experience for 11th- and 12th-grade students who work together for a three-period block of time during the school day. As developed at Carnegie-Mellon, the program includes grades 10, 11, and 12. However, the Exurbia adaptation does not include grade 10. Students enroll in specially designed courses in social studies, English, and physical education. They also participate in a special class period which stresses self-governance in carrying out a variety of civic-education experiences and projects. The special class, called a community meeting, meets for one three-hour period each week, and it begins after the first month of the school year. All students take the remainder of their courses with the general student body.

Based on the Carnegie-Mellon project, the program has five sets of goals which serve as the ". . . basis for structuring an innovative program which aims to expand traditional conceptions of civic education:
1. the development of basic participatory skills;
2. the development of basic intellectual skills;

3. personal development, including the development of self-knowledge, self-esteem, and personal identity;
4. development of the ability to understand democratic values (cognitive moral development); and
5. development of knowledge."

Again citing from a report from Carnegie-Mellon, "...the social studies courses deal with various ways in which individuals are organized into groups and examines different forms and functions of government. The English course presents literature with three themes — the individual, the individual in the wider community, and the organization in the community." Through their participation in the community-activities component of the course, "...students have an opportunity to relate the substantive content from the academic courses to their own needs and experiences as members of the civic-education community."

The CEDP also draws upon the six basic elements for a comprehensive project that were developed at Carnegie-Mellon. First, a comprehensive civic-education program must extend over several years of schooling, for only limited change in development can be expected in a one-year program. Second, the program must extend well beyond the social studies to include as many aspects of the school program as possible. Third, a civic-education program must change not only the formal classwork but also the hidden or latent curriculum involving the total of institutional arrangements. Fourth, a civic-education program must include an intensive, long-run, teacher-preparation program. Fifth, the program requires development of new curricular materials which provide sequential and cumulative learning experiences reflecting the psychological, philosophical, and educational rationale of the program. And finally, a comprehensive program of civic education must be carefully evaluated.

Not all of these elements are uniformly attained at Exurbia. For example, the CEDP is currently available for only two years. Since the program is limited to three hours in the morning sections, it is not clear how much impact the program has on the latent curriculum. Student-teacher relationships appear to be on a more nearly equal and less formal basis in civic-education classes, since teachers do not attempt to maintain as much strong control over all students. Classes frequently separate into smaller work groups, and at times it may seem that chaos reigns. Although students do not spend all their working time on the assigned tasks, the bulk of class time seems to be concerned with completing work assignments. Students also appear to develop strong and positive identifications with their teachers, which carry over into extracurricular activities.

Initiation and evolution of the program. The person responsible for introducing the now two-year-old Civic Education Developmental Program to Exurbia High School is the current assistant principal for curriculum. Several years ago he attended a presentation given by Professor Edwin Fenton, director of the civic education project at Carnegie-Mellon. He subsequently invited Fenton to visit Exurbia High School to conduct a faculty seminar. As a result of the interest generated by Professor Fenton, two Exurbia teachers, one in English and one in social studies, were given district support to participate in a fifteen-week teacher-training workshop held at Carnegie-Mellon University during the spring semester of 1977. While there, they were exposed to all aspects of the project, including the organization of English and social-studies courses, the use of Kohlberg moral dilemmas as a teaching and discussion technique, and the implementation of community meetings. They also observed the program in action at a number of high schools and worked with other student teachers in the modification of curricular materials for Exurbia High School.

The Exurbia school board provided funds to refurbish two classrooms for the large community meetings. Since the program would not use the regular English and social studies texts, the board also allocated $500 for the reproduction of curriculum materials. In addition, each CEDP teacher was given one extra free period during his or her regular schedule to be used for planning and coordinating course content and schedules. Although the CEDP includes English, social studies, and physical education, neither the activities nor the curriculum materials in the physical-education section are as well integrated into the program as English and social studies.

CEDP is assigned a three-hour block of time during morning sessions. These hours can be used flexibly by the teachers for any activities they deem appropriate so long as they do not extend beyond the allocated periods or intrude on any other aspects of the school schedule. The primary curriculum materials used in the courses are modifications of those developed at Carnegie-Mellon. Most modifications were made in the English curriculum, which was found to be too difficult for the Exurbia students.

Initial efforts to recruit students were undertaken in the spring of 1977, and one of the teachers returned briefly from Carnegie-Mellon to assist. The students were advised about the program through a descriptive pamphlet and an introductory assembly period. In the first year, more students enrolled for the course than could be accommodated, a phenomenon which has occurred in each subsequent year. Teachers in the program decided who would be turned away on the basis of their combined judgment as to who would benefit most from the program.

During the first year, a ten-week in-service seminar was offered by the CEDP staff to other Exurbia faculty as a normal part of each district's in-service teacher training program. It was also attended by faculty from three nearby high schools. The intent was not so much to recruit new teachers to the program as to arouse their interest and support and to share some of the civic-education program techniques. The seminar was uniformly reported to be successful by both the leaders and the attendees.

During the school year 1979-80, the CEDP is in its third year of operation. The program has undergone a number of minor modifications, the most significant being a change in staffing. There are now three teachers involved in the program: the director, who teaches English; a social-studies teacher, who joined the program in its second year of operation; and a physical-education teacher, a new member of the Exurbia faculty who transferred from a nearby school to work specifically in the CEDP program, having become interested in it through the teacher in-service seminar. During the summer of 1979, the director and the physical-education teacher participated in a summer-long seminar at CMU, again with district support.

In 1979-80 there were three sections of CEDP, averaging 23 students each. To be eligible for admission to the CEDP, students must be either in track 3 or track 4. An honors program is available for civic-education students to allow them to get track 4 credit for both the English and social-studies courses. A small proportion of exurbia students choose the course as an elective — almost one hundred of last year's graduating class of approximately 500 students had been involved in civic education.

As reported by both project staff and the Exurbia faculty at large, the course does not attract the most able students. There is apparently some competition among teachers at Exurbia for the more gifted students. Some faculty report that they have reservations about the quality of the academic work completed in the Civic Education Developmental Program. An example cited was a newspaper produced by the students during the academic year 1978-79. Several faculty felt that the paper had too many grammatical and technical errors to meet minimum standards for a high-school publication, even though they recognized that the emphasis in its production was on process rather than content.

It was also reported that a few teachers lead their very best students away from the CEDP, since some students who had dropped out of the program reported to the faculty that it was not sufficiently challenging. Other faculty took a completely neutral stand, believing the program should be available for interested students but doing little or nothing to encourage or discourage students from enrolling. Still other faculty reported that such procedures as giving small prizes for completing homework are not appropriate for the secondary-school level, and one faculty member indicated that maintaining control of the students in a relatively unstructured classroom was too onerous for a high-school teacher. On the other hand, it was clear that the administration and most faculty at Exurbia supported the program and felt that CEDP had obviously helped a number of students.

Students generally expressed positive attitudes toward CEDP, but there was some degree of disparity in enthusiasm. Students reported that most regular classes at Exurbia were boring, but they felt that the CEDP sessions were interesting. They indicated that it was easy to participate in discussions, each student being given ample opportunity and encouragement to speak out, since teachers did not assume a "supervisory" stance in the classroom. Some students objected strongly to the inaccuracy of a perception by their peers and faculty that the program was not very demanding, claiming they spent six to seven hours per week on outside preparation.

Prospects. The future of the Civic Education Developmental Program at Exurbia High School is very uncertain. The teachers involved in the program want to expand it to a three-year program to correspond to the Carnegie-Mellon model, but that seems unlikely. Average class size at Exurbia High is 38 students, and the average class size in the CEDP is 23. In order to expand the program, additional teacher time would have to be allocated to CEDP, causing increased class size for other courses. The administration at Exurbia High is concerned that the school board will impose another reduction in faculty and thereby force the cancellation of the CEDP. In fact, the Exurbia High administration came very close to withdrawing the program for the school year 1979-80, and it was only through the persistent efforts of the principal and assistant principal that it was possible to keep it alive.

The fiscal constraints which are affecting all educational institutions in the nation are present at Exurbia as well. Although the CEDP has in the past received different types of assistance from the school board, it is not known whether the board will have the resources available to continue support of the program in the future. Given the desire to keep it but the uncertainty which exists in the administration, there are no plans at the present time to change other aspects of the program's goals, contents, or procedures. In fact, it seems certain that in the immediate future tremendous efforts will be required on the part of the administration and faculty to keep the program intact.

Evaluation. As stated by the project staff at Carnegie-Mellon University, evaluation is the sixth key element in a comprehensive civic-education program. Evaluation is intended to assess student progress in all five goals — participatory skills, intellectual skills, personal development, democratic values, and knowledge.

Evaluation of the civic-education program at Exurbia High School is heavily dependent upon instruments and guidance provided by the staff at CMU. During the first and second year of the CEDP, the following evaluation activities were undertaken to measure attainment of the project goals:

1. Participatory skills
   The development of skills in reading, composition, and literature

was tested with the relevant Tests of Academic Progress. These paper-and-pencil instruments were administered to all students who enrolled in civic education. Pretests were given in September and posttests administered in June. The development of social studies skills was measured with the Sequential Tests of Educational Progress (STEP). Form 2A of STEP was administered in September, and Form 2B was administered in June. In both the first and second year, consistent and statistically significant differences were observed on these instruments.

2. Intellectual skills

A Piagetian Logic Test was used to assess student transition from concrete to formal operational thought. All students in the civic-education program took the same tests as a pretest and posttest instrument each year. Small and sometimes inconsistent differences were measured between the pre- and post-administrations, and it was not clear what impact participation in the program had produced on intellectual skills as measured with this instrument.

3. Personal Development

Two instruments were used to assess students' personal development. In both the first and second year, students were randomly divided into two groups. The first group was administered the Coopersmith Self-Esteem Inventory and the remaining students took the Rotter Sentence Blank Completion Test. Both tests were administered as pretests and posttests during the first and second years. Some gains were detected with these instruments, but the magnitude was disappointing to the CEDP staff.

4. Democratic values

The Kohlberg Moral Judgment Interview was used to measure student development in this area. Because the administration and scoring of the interviews is very time-consuming, a one-third sample was selected representing sex, race, and ethnic distributions of all students in the program. The interviews were administered only to the sample. Form A was administered in September and Form B administered to the same students in June of each year. Again, small gains in moral-development scores were observed; average student change in both years was less than one-half of one stage on the Kohlberg scale.

5. Knowledge

The Cooperative Social-Studies Test for Senior High School American History was administered to measure student progress in this area. Pretests and posttests were administered in both years, and statistically significant differences were obtained in both administrations.

During the second year of operation of the Civic Education Developmental Program, there was a total of 11 students taking the program for a second year. Comparisons were made between the pretest scores in September of 1977 and posttest scores in June of 1979 for this small group of students. Statistically significant differences were obtained with the Tests of Academic Progress, the personal development instruments, and the Cooperative Social-Studies Test; not for the Piagetian Logic Test. But perhaps the most dramatic changes were in the Kohlberg Moral Judgment Interview. The average student gain was 1.25 stages.

All instruments were administered to the students by the Exurbia High School staff, and forwarded to Carnegie-Mellon for processing and analyzing. Personnel at both Exurbia and Carnegie are most enthusiastic about the results obtained thus far, particularly those from the small sample of students who have been in the program for two years. There appears to be fairly strong evidence that the impact of the CEPD really does not occur until students have been exposed to the program for a two-year period.

Several additional efforts have been made at an assessment of the CEDP during its second year of operation. Sixty items were drawn from the citizenship instrument of the National Assessment of Education Progress and administered at the end of the year. Finally, a locally devised written subjective evaluation form was completed by all students in the program during the second year. The students were asked to identify in their own words the components of the program that they found most and least valuable. CEDP staff found these materials useful, but they did not know how to accomplish further analyses of the students' comments.

During the 1978-79 school year, the second year of the CEDP, an intern spent six weeks at the school working with the program. The intern was a graduate student in education at a nearby state college and undertook several tasks related to the CEDP. She compiled a number of sociograms depicting friendship, leadership, and academic excellence networks among Exurbia's civic-education program students. She also administered a "locus-of-control" test and reported that no difference existed on it between CEDP students and a sample of other Exurbia students. Although she was asked to keep participation records based on classroom observations, she never finished this task. After completing her internship she submitted a strongly negative formative evaluation report on the CEDP. The staff never perceived her as an evaluator, and they were disappointed with what they considered a naive assessment of the program.

During the third year of operation of the CEDP, all instruments previously administered are again being used in evaluation activities. However, the evaluation design will be expanded to include the administration of these instruments to a small sample of Exurbia students who have not previously or are not currently enrolled in the CEDP. Since students for the program are self-selected, the comparison will not involve randomized assignment to experimental and control groups. Nevertheless, the extension of the evaluation to include students not enrolled in the program can shed further light on the effectiveness and impact of the program. In addition, there are currently 18 students taken the CEDP for their second year, and it will be possible to assess again the impact of the program, comparing those students who have been in it for one year with those in the program for a two-year period. When all evaluation materials have been collected and analyzed after the third year of operation, a summary report of all evaluation activities is planned for submission to the Exurbia School Board. All involved in the program at Exurbia High School and Carnegie-Mellon University expect that the results of the evaluation will provide a convincingly strong reason for continuation and perhaps expansion of the program.

A Values Clarification Program in Midcity

The setting. Midcity is a community of 50,000 people, located on the West Coast about 20 miles from a major metropolitan center. For decades, it had been a largely white though ethnically heterogeneous city, but not long after World War II it became attractive to professionals and to minority families who were moving out from the metropolis. It is now rather sharply divided into two parts: a working-class section, mostly of older residents and still mostly White but now with a substantial proportion of Black and Hispanic families; and a white-collar section (even more heavily White but with a scattering of Black families) which is relatively affluent and tends to be liberal in politics, and which is dominant in civic affairs. All told, about 15 percent of the populatrion is Black, 5 percent Hispanic, and the rest White but of many different ethnic groups.

The city's newspaper, generally conservative in tone, had been running editorials for some time deploring the "decline of morality." Ministers delivered sermons on the same subject. No one suggested that this was a matter for the schools to deal with. However, about five years ago a new superintendent arrived in Midcity. He shared the concerns about morality, but he believed that the schools did have an obligation to help students deal with moral issues, and after a year or two on the scene he came to feel that the community would be receptive to some action on his part. He decided to initiate a program but to move cautiously.

The schools. Midcity has two high schools, each accommodating about half its student population of 3,000 in grades 10-12. South High, the older and for a long time the only high school in the city, is in the working-class section. It is a conventional school building, well kept but showing its age. The staff enjoys considerable seniority and follows conventional teaching techniques for the most part. There is general agreement among the townspeople and within the school system administration that the teachers are highly competent. For the past ten years or more, about two-thirds of the students have gone on to some form of postsecondary education; nearly 15 percent of the seniors attend a county vocational school. Students have displayed intense loyalty to the school; the high proportion returning for 25th reunions is often remarked upon.

North High School, serving the white-collar section, was built less than ten years ago — a single-story, campus-like plant, carpeted, with broad expanses of glass and movable walls. Its staff is younger and more experimental, but it has been a stable group and has won the respect of parents and students. The proportion of graduates going on to college is only a little higher than in South High, but North's students are more likely to go to the prestigious institutions.

Initiation of the program. The superintendent had certain philosophical convictions about the nature of a moral education program. He believed that moral education was so important that it should suffuse the entire curriculum rather than be restricted to one or two courses on the subject. He also believed that it was improper for the public schools to teach any one "brand" of morality, but that the broad goal of instruction should be rather to help students learn how to make moral decisions for themselves while being "neutral" about the content of those decisions. Finally, he believed that moral education was so sensitive a topic that teachers had to be allowed to handle it in their own way. When he read about values clarification in one of the professional journals to which he subscribed, it seemed to him that it could meet all of these criteria, and he decided to take steps to have it introduced into Midcity's high schools.

The superintendent also had certain pragmatic convictions about strategies for getting an innovation adopted, the most important of which were that an innovation could not succeed if it were imposed upon teachers by fiat and that — especially in an area such as moral education — it has to pay reasonable attention to community sentiments. Consequently, his first step was to form a committee of teachers, parents, and students to "explore the question of the schools' responsibility with respect to education in moral decision making." He met with the committee at its first meeting and mentioned that he would be glad to arrange for a visit by a staff member of the National Humanistic Education Center, who would discuss with the committee the Center's views on and experience in moral education at the secondary level. His choice of the NHEC was, of course, not random; it is the center of development and activity for the values-clarification approach.

The committee was much impressed by the speaker from NHEC, and it did not explore other approaches to moral education. In its report, it recommended that moral education be adopted as a goal for Midcity's high schools, and it proposed the following objectives, which drew heavily on wording found in values-clarification materials:

—to encourage students to make choices, and to make them freely;

—to help them discover and examine available alternatives when faced with choices;

—to help them weigh alternatives thoughtfully, reflecting on the consequences of each;

—to encourage them to consider what it is that they prize and cherish;

—to give them opportunities to make public affirmations of their choices;

—to encourage them to act, behave, and live in accordance with their choices;

—to help them to examine repeated behaviors or patterns in their lives.

The report, which was distributed to all high-school teachers, also presented sample instructional materials and a bibliography, whose indebtedness to the values-clarification literature was again quite clear. The committee recommended that the superintendent arrange for a workshop on moral education to be conducted by the NHEC staff and to be offered to all high-school teachers but obligatory for none. The superintendent was quite happy to follow these recommendations. The sums of money involved were small enough to be covered by discretionary funds he had at his disposal, and he saw no need to bring the matter before the school board.

Ther workshop was held the following summer. Twelve teachers attended, most of them from English and social studies but one in science and one in Spanish. They learned about values clarification and devised materials for their own use. They were uniformly enthusiastic about the experience, and 10 of them said at the end that they intended to devote some time to values clarification in their classroom during the coming year. At their request, a considerable volume of material was purchased from NHEC. The superintendent engaged the workshop leader as a consultant to be available for phone consultation during the academic year; later, he reported that he had had only two calls.

Evolution and operation of the program. Since the use of values clarification was voluntary on the part of teachers, and since it was not confined to any single course, it was difficult to know just how widely it was actually being used. In a memo to the teachers who had attended the workshop, the superintendent asked that they file reports at the end of the year concerning their experience. Nine teachers complied, five from North High and four from South. The reports ranged from bare two-sentence statements to five-page encomiums. One teacher, who had been teaching a course on American Politics, primarily with materials supplied by the Constitutional Rights Foundation, said she had made almost daily use of values clarification in order to emphasize the connections between morality and political decision making. A history teacher spoke of having restructured even the "cognitive" parts of his course as a result of the introduction of values clarification. Several teachers commented that values clarification could well be extended to the elementary grades.

As he was reading the reports, the superintendent began to suspect that some of them were written only to please him, and he realized that he had no independent means of verifying what was said in them. (He had thought of visiting some classrooms of the teachers who had attended the workshop, but he did not want to appear to be too insistent on the use of values clarification, and he knew he could not even be sure when any given teacher was going to use it.) For this reason, and also because of their great variability and the difficulty of generalizing from them, he found the reports to be less useful than he had thought they would be. Nevertheless, he continued to ask for them out of concern that to do otherwise might be taken as a sign that he was no longer interested. He determined to seek some help, before the second year began, in learning more about what was happening in the program and what effects it was having.

The principal at North High seemed to welcome values clarification in his school more actively than did his counterpart at South High. Perhaps because he believed that increased student responsibility would provide more occasions for the use of values clarification and would enhance its effects as well — but perhaps because he was inclined in this direction anyway and values clarification furnished a pretext — he took such steps as eliminating hall passes and study halls and even the fixed lunch hours, so that students had to make many more choices than they'd had to before. He consulted with the Student Council more often and gave it wider scope for decision making. At his encouragement, the Student Council named two of its members to attend meetings of the School Board, and they even made occasional presentations at those meetings. It also formed a Student Court to "try" minor cases, but its jurisdiction was vague and no cases were ever brought before it. Perhaps stimulated by the principal's actions, one of the guidance counselors at North High began to use values-clarification techniques in small-group sessions with students who were having academic difficulties.

There was little overt community reaction to the introduction of values clarification. A few parents did protest to the school board over the use of one discussion question that had been suggested in the values-clarification materials. It presented students with a hypothetical case in which their spouse and their best friend had become attracted to each other and asked students to state whether they would prefer that the two continue the relationship secretly, or that they continue the relationship but "be honest" about it, or that the spouse ask for a divorce. Some of the parents pointed out that another possible preference, that the relationship be broken off, was not mentioned, while others argued that the question was not even an appropriate one for discussion by high-school students. At the request of the school board, the principal informed the teacher in whose class the incident had occurred that it had been poor judgment to use the question, and nothing more was heard about it. The city's newspaper never printed an editorial congratulating the school system — or criticizing it — for dealing with moral issues, nor did the superintendent receive any calls or visits from members of the clergy.

The NHEC ran workshops again each of the next two summers, and about ten teachers attended each one. Values clarification seemed to be well on the way to becoming a routine part of instruction; and since it required only a minimal amount of funds, there appeared to be no obstacle to that. However, in the middle of the third year, the superintendent accepted an appointment in another city, and without his personal support, the future of the program is uncertain.

Evaluation. When the superintendent realized that he was not getting the information he had hoped for from the teachers' reports, he asked the director of testing to plan and implement a more systematic evaluation. The director objected that the evaluation should have been designed *before* the program was put into operation, and that she had little extra time and no staff to do the work, but she agreed to do the best she could.

The director of testing quickly discovered that she had been given a very difficult task. The report of the teacher-parent-student committee had said nothing about evaluation; and when the testing director read over the goals that were recommended in the report, she found that they referred primarily to classroom processes rather than student outcomes, and she did not have nearly enough resources to permit intensive classroom observations. The student behaviors that were mentioned could hardly be measured: "How can I tell whether students are considering what they 'prize and cherish'?" Conversations with teachers revealed that the problem of evaluation had not been raised in the workshop, either, and that the teachers could express their own expectations of values clarification only vaguely, often in the form of examples rather than general statements. A phone call to the NHEC consultant produced no help; he advised against the use of paper-and-pencil instruments but he offered no alternative.

While doing some reading on the subject of moral education, the testing director came across a description of Kohlberg's Moral Judgment Interview (MJI), and she decided to try it. Even though she knew that the MJI had not been designed to measure whatever sorts of changes might occur through the use of values clarification (which after all did not posit any developmental stages), it seemed to her that the intentions of the two approaches were sufficiently similar to warrant its use, and the NHEC consultant agreed. By the end of the year, she had managed to arrange half a dozen interviews with students in classes where the teachers were making frequent use of values clarification. All of the interviews were with North High students. The students' responses struck her as being on the whole more "mature" than she had expected, but she was not sure how to interpret that. It might have been attributable to the effects of value clarification, but the students may have been that way before any exposure to values clarification, or, if they had indeed changed, it might have been because of the increased student autonomy at North and not because of values clarification at all. Indeed, the seemingly high maturity level may have been the result of nothing more than her own low expectations of what she would find (she had no frame of reference by which to judge what she heard from the students), or it might simply have been an erroneous impression, for she found it impossible to apply the scoring procedure rigorously to the interviews she had done. In any event, she was reluctant to draw any inferences from a mere half-dozen interviews, and yet she did not have time to do more of them.

Despite the NHEC consultant's advice, she did try to write some paper-and-pencil items, with multiple-choice answers, because it was the sort of thing she was familiar with. But she soon realized that it would be all too easy for students to choose the answer they thought was "expected," whatever their "real" answer might be. She next made an effort to devise some unobtrusive measures. There had been reports of students' lockers being broken into, so she thought that the trend in the number of such incidents might reflect the effects (or lack of effects) of values clarification. However, the number of reported break-ins per week or even per month was too small to show any reliable trend, and she was not sure that all of the break-ins were being reported or that all the reports were factual. Moreover, some students told her that, after hearing about the break-ins, students generally were using their lockers less, which would mean that there was less temptation to break into them. Another idea she had was to find out how many hours students spent doing volunteer work for public-service organizations, and to compare the average number of hours spent by students who were and were not enrolled in classes where values clarification was being used. She asked several teachers to gather such information from their students, but most of the teachers were unenthusiastic about doing it, and after a while she stopped making the requests.

The conversations she had with teachers in the course of this last effort, however, often were enlightening. For one thing, she learned that only half of the teachers who had attended the workshops were making any regular use of values-clarification techniques. Those who were using them told her of what they thought their failures and successes had been, and they suggested ways in which the use of the techniques could be improved. The testing director felt that the materials from these conversations were the most valuable part of her report to the superintendent.

The latter, after getting permission from the testing director, sent a copy of the report to the NHEC consultant for his use in preparing the next workshop, and the consultant did indeed find that it helped him gain a sense of the realities of the program.

An Actionist Program at John Dewey High School

The setting. Westmount is a manufacturing and commercial center in the Midwest, with a population of 250,000. The city has been stable in size for two decades or more, but the proportion of minorities among its residents has been growing; its population is now about 20 percent Black and 5 percent Hispanic, with a substantial number of Southeast Asian refugees as well. A major unit of the state university is located in the city, which also has a long tradition as a cultural center and is the seat of the most populous county in the state. It thus has a highly diversified economy.

The school. Among the six high schools in Westmount is John Dewey, a 15-year-old, one-story building arranged in a square around a courtyard. It was built for a student body of 2,000, but now has an enrollment of only 1,500, because another high school was recently erected to serve part of its former attendance district. The ethnic composition of the student body is similar to that of the city as a whole, except that the school accommodates all the Southeast Asian students, by virtue of a multilingual, multicultural program which it offers on behalf of the school system. The faculty of 90 full-time instructors is predominantly White, though there are also a few part-time teachers' aides of Asian background in the multilingual program. The faculty has an average teaching experience of 10 years and is regarded as competent if traditional. The principal was appointed to her position seven years ago; she had been brought in from outside the system by the then superintendent, who urged her to seek out ways of "shaking the school up a little." The principal was happy to comply — she was energetic and ambitious and had firm convictions about the leadership role of a high-school principal.

Initiation of the program. One of the innovations the principal had in mind was some form of moral education. She had long believed that the schools had badly neglected the affective side of their students' education and she wanted to do something to strengthen it, without being quite sure of what the best method would be.

The local unit of the state university had a Center for Youth Action and Research (CYAR), whose director had a national reputation as a leader in the development of the concept of action learning. He became acquainted with the principal not long after her arrival in Westmount and began to urge upon her the merits of action learning. Getting students out into the "real world" of the community, he argued, would not only help them learn certain social and technical skills which could not be learned in the classroom, but would also make them more receptive to classroom learning, when they say how relevant it actually was. When he became aware of the principals's concern for moral education, he added that action learning had the potential of developing students' moral sensitivities as well, because their actions would have more serious consequences for other people than is commonly the case in the school. Westmount, he pointed out, had in abundance the kinds of community resources that could make an action-learning program successful.

The CYAR was already involved in a few small-scale efforts at other schools, but the director suggested that it and John Dewey now cooperate in a major school-wide program. He felt sure that it would be possible to obtain a grant for this purpose from a private foundation, a prospect which was attractive to the principal because of the visibility and prestige that would accompany such a grant. They talked the idea over with the superintendent and the John Dewey Parents Council and were given strong support for moving ahead, although the principal had the impression that the members of the Parents Council were interpreting action learning to mean primarily job preparation.

The foundation proposal which the director and the principal wrote covered all the possibilities, speaking of the "potential impact on students' intellectual, social, moral, personal, and career development." The way of achieving these goals was to be to place students "in a *real* arena, with *real* choices and *real* consequences." The proposal called for working with six interested teachers to help them provide relevant action-learning opportunities to the students in their classes, while a maximum of 30 seniors would be permitted to devote their entire schedule to action learning for one semester. The section on evaluation referred to the Moral Judgment Interview, the Defining Issues Test, "and other appropriate measures," without making clear how these would be used. The project was given the title REAL (Resources for Education and Active Learning). The foundation to which the proposal was submitted made a grant of $195,000 to support the project for three years.

Operation and evolution of the program. A large part of the foundation grant went to release a teacher for three-quarters of her time to serve as project director and placement coordinator. This proved to be insufficient, and in the second year, this teacher was made project director full time and another teacher was released for half time to help in locating placement sites. The director was responsible for the group of seniors who were engaged in Project REAL full time, and she was also ultimately responsible for finding placements for the other students who were involved in action learning only as part of one of the courses they were taking. However, her half-time assistant, the CYAR director and his staff, the participating teachers, and indeed the students themselves found some of the action-learning placements. Both the CYAR director and the Project REAL director met with the participating teachers as a group at the beginning of each semester and consulted with them individually from time to time.

Finding suitable placements for action learning proved to be the program's chief problem. The director-coordinator wanted to "match" each student with a suitable action-learning site, but she gradually realized that there were no clear criteria for what a "good match" was. Furthermore, whenever she received an offer from a site to accommodate a student, she found herself trying to persuade *some* student to take advantage of it rather than having it lost to the program project. At first, all of the placements were with governmental agencies or nonprofit organizations — a veterans' hospital, a county nursing home, the city council, several museums, the elementary schools, the Red Cross and the Y's — but by the beginning of the second year that restriction was dropped. It was difficult to argue that, so far as benefits to a student were concerned, providing services in a county nursing home was different from providing them in a proprietary nursing home, or that helping out in a museum gift shop was different from helping out in a gift shop that was not located in a museum.

By the beginning of the third year, it became apparent that there was a "core" of half a dozen sites that could be relied on to provide placements for eight or ten students every year; the rest of the sites stayed with the program for a year or two and then had to be replaced. Thus, a great deal of time continued to be spent in finding suitable placements. The uncertainties were especially troublesome for the seniors who were engaged in Project REAL full time. The half-time coordinator who was added the second year was a former Outward Bound instructor, and he filled part of the gap by organizing a three-week trip to a nearby national park as part of the schedule for those full-time students who were interested. This quickly became one of the most popular parts of the program. On the other hand, it also became the target of disparaging remarks from several teachers who believed that Project REAL was undermining the importance of classroom learning. They used the image of a "bunch of kids running around the countryside" to criticize the entire program, even though the coordinator made a serious effort to emphasize the learning aspects of the trip — e.g., by giving the students responsibility for making detailed plans before leaving, and by bringing them together for a half-day discussion when it was over.

Part of the problem in finding and keeping suitable placements lay in maintaining good relationships with the adult at the site who was responsible for the students' activities there. It was usually through the interest and cooperation of some individual that a site became available to the program, and as long as that individual was there and kept his or her interest, the site would remain available. Sometimes, however, these people would leave for other employment, or would be disappointed by the students' work or reliability, or would find that they did not have enough time to devote to the student, and in such cases the site would usually drop out of the program. The director had intended to visit every placement site and talk to the supervisor there at least once a year, but there was not nearly enough time for that. She did send a one-page flyer about the project to the supervisors when they first joined it, but it said little about what the school expected of them (the director herself was not sure what the expectations were). The flyer did not mention the moral-education objectives at all, because the director could not devise a way of stating them without sounding pretentious. From talking to students, the director learned that the supervisors interpreted their role in quite different ways, especially in terms of the amount of explicit instruction they gave to the students, but that by and large they tended to emphasize narrowly relevant job skills. The lack of adequate communications with the supervisors remained one of the director's major dissatisfactions with the project.

Students' activities at the placement sites varied widely. Sometimes they were put to work at routine tasks and were essentially like cheap, unskilled labor. In other places, they were given duties that they lacked either the skill or the time to perform. At a few places, there really was nothing for the student to do. At the suggestion of the director, some of the teachers gave their Project REAL students assignments to be carried out at their placement sites, such as developing an organization chart or describing the decision-making process, but students complained that it was difficult for them to get access to the needed information and that sometimes carrying out the assignments interfered with meeting their work responsibilities. Another problem was that it was rarely possible to place more than one student at a site, and as a result students sometimes said they felt "isolated." Nevertheless, most students enjoyed their placement activities and felt that most of the time they were doing interesting things that were useful to themselves and others.

Getting students to the placement sites and back was another problem. Soon after the project began, the director started getting complaints from other teachers that Project REAL students were missing too much class time. She was then able to get authorization to use some of the grant funds to buy a van and hire a school-bus driver to use it to transport students. That worked reasonably well, but when the foundation grant expired at the end of three years, it was no longer financially feasible. The students then had to get to and from the placement sites themselves, and that created several difficulties: It meant that students were again out of school for more hours, that sometimes they missed appointments, and that some placement sites had to be dropped because they were inaccessible by public transportation and many students did not have use of a car.

The in-school side of the program was never fully developed. The proposal said that all of the participating students would be brought together once a week to discuss moral and interpersonal problems that may have arisen during the Project REAL activities, but scheduling difficulties made that impossible for those students who were participating only as part of a course. The full-time seniors did meet regularly, but the sessions turned out to be less productive than had been thought. The students' placements and experiences were so varied that it was difficult for them to understand one another's accounts without lengthy descriptions — which no one was interested in hearing. Even when a problem was raised for discussion, the director, who presided at these meetings, did not know how to handle it or what to suggest. When scheduling difficulties began to interfere with these meetings, too, she gradually let them peter out. However, she did maintain a one-week "orientation" session for the seniors at the beginning of each semester, before the students began their outside placements; at these sessions, the director talked to them and with them about what to expect, what their obligations were, and what to look out for. Some students, impatient to get out into the "real world," complained that these orientation sessions took too much time.

Despite all the problems and shortcomings, Project REAL appeared to be very popular with students and with parents. At meetings of the school board and parents' groups, the principal occasionally found that she had to remind people of the value of conventional classroom activity — that there were, after all, many important things that could not be learned at any possible combination of placement sites. Not only were there more students at Dewey wanting to participate in the program than could be accommodated, but students from other schools were also seeking to enroll. For a while, the principal at Dewey tried to include them, but the staff objected. The principal suggested to her counterparts at other schools that they contribute to the administrative costs of the program; some did, while others responded by refusing to allow their students to participate any longer.

When the foundation grant expired, Project REAL was kept in operation with the school district's own funds for a year. On the basis of the experience with the project, the school then applied for and received a grant under the federal Youth Employment and Demonstration Projects Act, which allowed it to keep the part-time component of the project in operation. To qualify for the grant, however, the project had to be presented as one whose explicit objective was career preparation. The principal experienced a twinge of disappointment at this transformation, since her original goal had been one of moral education, but she was convinced that not only had she brought an innovation to the school — one that surely was useful in its own right — but also that, as a byproduct of their experience in Project REAL and its successor, students would gain in moral sensitivity.

Evaluation. Among her other duties, the project director was supposed to conduct the evaluation studies that were promised in the proposal. The CYAR director assigned a graduate student to help her. During the first year, the project director had little time for this aspect of her job. Participating students were told to keep a journal of events at their placement sites and reflections about them, and they were to turn this in, together with a self-evaluation of their participation, at the end of the semester. The project director glanced at them but wasn't sure what to do with them or how to evaluate them; they remained in her desk drawer, but believing that she would have more time to study them in the second year, she asked students again to keep journals and write self-evaluations. The graduate student had meanwhile administered the Moral Judgment Interview to a few Project REAL students, but they complained that it seemed irrelevant and it was dropped.

During the second year, the project director, together with the graduate student, made more extensive efforts at collecting evaluative evidence. They devised a rating form to be completed by teachers, in which the latter were asked to rate the students in their classes on such characteristics as "sense of responsibility" and "consideration for others." They asked the teachers participating in Project REAL to fill out these forms for each of their students toward the end of the term, and they compared the ratings given to project students with the ratings given to students in the same classes who had not taken part in the project. There did not seem to be any differences, although the graduate student pointed out that this was not a valid measure of project effects since there were no comparable ratings for the students at the beginning of the semester. The project director was certain that teachers would balk at filling out these forms twice each term, at the beginning and at the end, so in the third year they asked teachers whether students "showed more responsibility at the end of the term than they did at the beginning." They were not at all sure that teachers could recall such things accurately, but in any event, there were again no differences between the ratings given to participating and nonparticipating students. A similar questionnaire sent to parents produced similar results.

During the second year, they also administered the Defining Issues Test to all seniors who were enrolled in Project REAL full time in the first semester, to all the students in a senior English class which was concentrating on literary works dealing with issues of wealth and poverty, and to a senior class in Problems in Democracy. Again, there appeared to be no difference, though once more there was no measure of any *change* that might have taken place.

In the end, the project director found that the most convincing evidence came from conversations with the participating students. Even

95

though they were haphazard and unstructured, there was a consistent and conspicuous absence of any references to, or even perceptions of, the moral dimensions of their placement activities. The students talked about their activities almost entirely in terms of the skills they were learning and the attitudes they were acquiring toward particular kinds of jobs and kinds of workplaces. When this began to become clear, she went back to the students' journals to read them more carefully, and she found that they confirmed this impression. Indeed, when she re-read the original proposal, she realized that this point of view might even have been implicit in the project from the very start, in its emphasis on the workplace as the "real world." By virtue of this accumulation of various sorts of clues, even though no one of them was conclusive, she felt confident in concluding her evaluation report by saying that moral growth could not be counted on to occur as a byproduct of other activities. A program whose goal is moral growth must deal with moral issues explicitly and directly.

A Rationalist Program at Central City High School

The setting. The community served by Central City High School is near the downtown business and financial district of a large mid-Atlantic urban complex. The neighborhood was socially heterogeneous until the mid-1960s, when it began a radical transformation. The substantially White, ethnic, working-class population moved to suburban areas, and the community became more sharply divided along racial and economic dimensions. There is now a large minority population living in a public housing project located approximately two miles from Central High. Construction at the project started in the late 1940s, and there are now more than a dozen high-rise buildings in the area, some of which have deteriorated so badly that they are no longer habitable. The project has been the site of a number of racial incidents in recent years, including battles with the city police and sniping attacks. Local taxi drivers are leery of driving to the project even in daylight hours.

Approximately 50 percent of the current students at Central come from the housing project. Much of the original neighborhood, which has undergone substantial urban renewal, is now populated with primarily White, affluent executive and professional residents who work in center-city. The urban renewal, which escalated the price of housing beyond the means of the former working-class occupants, contributed to their exodus to the suburban areas. Some refurbished apartments, houses, and new condominiums in the Central City High School neighborhood are now selling in excess of several hundred thousand dollars. In addition, a recently court-ordered busing program to bring about racial balance throughout the city school system has produced further White flight to the suburbs.

The parents in the new affluent neighborhood have younger children, and there is a resurgence of activity among this group for improving the local public elementary schools. However, these efforts have focused *only* on the elementary schools; there is no organized constituency of secondary school students' parents to take an active interest in Centrals' programs.

The school. Corresponding to the recent transformation of the neighborhood, Central High School has also undergone substantial changes. In the mid-1960s at its peak enrollment, there were over 3,000 students, and approximately 30 percent came from White, working-class families. In the current school year, there are only 930 students, and almost all are minority-group members who live either in the housing project or other local, sub-standard housing. Sixty-five percent of the students are Black and 30 percent are Spanish-speaking; but the staff is almost 100 percent White. The decline in enrollment and the change in racial composition of the student population are attributable in large measure to both the urban renewal and the subsequent White exodus.

Central is considered one of several "problem high schools" in the city school district. Because the sale and use of drugs are commonplace occurrences within the school building and students and teachers have been the victims of violent attacks, police officers are regularly assigned to duty at the school, and patrol cars are in evidence throughout the neighborhood to prevent or control disturbances.

The school has a high drop-out rate. The entering ninth-grade class averages 300 students, but only about 80 seniors graduate each year. In addition to students dropping out upon reaching the maximum school age, there is also a high transfer rate as residents escape the deteriorating conditions at the housing project. Despite the transformation in the neighborhood and the changes in the student body at Central, the staff has remained comparatively stable. As the enrollment declined, the number of staff also diminished, but primarily as a result of the decision not to replace transfers and retirements. There are currently 70 faculty at Central.

The academic program is organized into six departments: science-mathematics, English, bilingual studies, business and vocational studies, physical education, and the social sciences (which include history, art, and music). The course under consideration here, Law and Society, is an elective in the social-sciences department.

The program — Law and Society. With financial support from Title IV-C of the Elementary and Secondary Education Act as administered by the State Board of Education and the city school board, the Law and Society course was initiated in the 1975-76 academic year. The basic structure, goals, and core curricula materials are identical for both experimental and control groups, but course activities are significantly enhanced in the experimental group. The course consists of six sections

— three experimental groups and three control groups. Approximately $30,000 are expended each year in the experimental sections for additional curriculum materials, field trips, secretarial support, and time in the program director's schedule for planning and evaluating class activities.

The original grant proposal included the following statement of goals:

> Interested students in grades 10, 11, and 12 will be enrolled in experimental and control sections of the Law and Society course at Central High School. After 39 weeks of treatment, students in the experimental section will increase their knowledge significantly (alpha .05) when compared to the control group as ascertained by a pre-and posttest of law knowledge.

The explicit intent of the program, then, is to produce cognitive changes in students. There was no statement to the effect that students would be more likely to adopt more positive attitudes toward self or toward legal agencies or less likely to become involved in deviant behavior as a consequence of participation in the experimental sections, but it does seem clear from discussions with program staff and from the materials used in the course that there is an implicit goal that students who participate in the additional activities of the experimental sections will experience positive attitudinal changes and also achieve higher probability of becoming law-abiding citizens. In discussing the program, teachers and administrators frequently claim with a great deal of pride that they can clearly recognize dramatic enhancements in positive self-concept and consistent shifts toward more favorable and supportive views of law enforcement agencies and personnel. Staff at Central High School are confident that these attitudinal changes will result in reduced incidence of future delinquent and criminal behaviors.

An additional implicit goal is derived from the fact that the project is supported by the Elementary and Secondary School Education Act. If at the end of the grant period it is demonstrated that students in the experimental group show evidence of "statistically significant differences" in legal knowledge compared with the control group, the program can be "validated" and thereby adopted for statewide dissemination. In practice, this means that the project director would be released from all teaching responsibilities for a one-year period to conduct in-service training throughout the state for similar law courses in other school systems.

The major activities to meet the program's goals consist of the following:

1. A teacher trained in the use of law-related curriculum materials and teaching strategies instructs in the experimental law classes that meet 40 minutes per day for 39 weeks. Units covered include

criminal law, civil law, and student rights and responsibilities.

2. Students interact with resource personnel from local criminal-justice agencies including police officers, prosecutors, judges, defense attorneys, and correctional officers. These interactions usually consist of a day-long visit by a student who "follows an adult's working day" and has an opportunity to gain some insight into routine activities.

3. Students participate in field experiences at local criminal-justice agencies including police departments, juvenile detention centers, courts, and prisons. Small groups of students, usually four to six, make field trips to particular agencies. They are usually given a tour of the entire facility and have an opportunity to observe the normal activities in each agency.

4. Students participate in 10 workshops. Topics include school violence and vandalism, juvenile delinquency, police procedures, trial procedures, and incarceration. The workshops are jointly planned and led by both teachers and students. They are usually convened as after-school activities and frequently involve the use of audiovisual materials, simulations, games, and presentations by adults from local criminal-justice agencies.

In addition, students participate in the following activities:

1. conducting classroom mock trials,

2. producing a law-related newspaper,

3. organizing and hosting workshops for other high-school students,

4. interacting with adults and students in school and community organizations,

5. engaging in peer- and cross-age teaching activities, conducting lessons and activities for students at the high-, middle-, and elementary-school levels,

6. attending workshops to be exposed to various teaching strategies (i.e., role playing, use of simulations, etc.), and

7. preparing learning packets on various law-related topics that may be used by other students.

Class size is a difficult statistic to cite for the Law and Society course, because student enrollment in all courses at Central City High decreases substantially as the academic year progresses. A large number of Central students drop out of school as soon as they reach the age of 16; others seek alternate programs. The typical junior or senior class starts in the fall with 35 students enrolled. By the end of the school year, there are usually only 20 students still formally enrolled in the course, and somewhere between 15 and 18 regularly attend class.

The primary texts used in the Law and Society course are two books on civil and criminal law produced by the Constitutional Rights Foundation, based in Los Angeles. CRF is a nonprofit, legal-education organization established in 1972. The various programs of CRF introduce legal studies in public and private schools throughout the nation, primarily at the secondary level. CRF programs develop and disseminate teaching materials to support law and education curricula. In addition, the staff provide training for teachers and technical assistance in program operations. The materials include textbooks on criminal and civil justice, newsletters, teacher manuals, and simulation and games. Although the program began in southern California, it has spread throughout the country, and there are several regional offices in the Midwest and on the East Coast.

By the time they complete the course, students in both the experimental and control sections are supposed to have read most of the material in the two primary texts. The experimental sections have access to a variety of other materials, some of which come from the Constitutional Rights Foundation and some from other sources, such as Prentice-Hall, Guidance Associates, Scholastic Book Services, Social Studies School Service, and others listed in the American Bar Association catalog of instructional materials for law-related education. Teachers in both the experimental and control sections use local newspapers to supplement these materials.

Students are required to complete three social-studies courses to meet graduation requirements at Central, and two of these courses must be in United States history. The law course is the most popular elective, and 80 to 85 percent of each graduating class have taken the course at some point. Since the course is optional, the students are self-selected, but their assignment to the experimental or control sections is made by the central scheduling office for the entire city school system. Neither students nor teachers have any input to this assignment process. The students indicate in the spring of each year their choices of courses for the subsequent academic year. These choices are then fed into a computer program which makes all section assignments. The main considerations in assignment are scheduling problems. In the absence of any detailed knowledge of the course scheduling algorithm, the program staff assume that randomized assignment is accomplished through this process. Several years ago, a comparison of reading scores between experimental and control groups by sex and race revealed minor differences. Whether there are any other systematic biases in assignment is unknown and, furthermore, beyond the control of the program staff. Given the fact that potential schedule conflict is the primary criterion in assignment of students to the experimental and control sections, it is quite likely that the patterns of other courses which students are taking are related to the assignment. If so, serious biases might creep into what is otherwise accepted as a randomized procedure, and individual differences might be more strongly related to the pattern of academic courses in which students enroll rather than any activities in the experimental sections.

The Law and Society course enjoys a great deal of support from the administration, faculty, and students. Among the latter, it has the reputation of being an interesting course as opposed to many others which are considered dull and routine. Furthermore, the experimental sections of the course can earn even stronger support. Students and faculty alike realize that they are engaged in a variety of unusual out-of-school activities; hence the students express a strong interest in the experimental group. All students in the Law and Society course are apparently highly regarded by their fellow students, faculty, and the administration. One of the students in the experimental section attained considerable recognition for winning a city-wide public speaking contest. The mayor presented the first-place prize, and the event was covered in the daily newspapers. The faculty were particularly proud of this student, who was apparently somewhat shy and withdrawn before becoming involved in the course.

The faculty, with very few exceptions, tends to support the course. Problems occur only when students begin to miss too many other classes as a result of their visits to outside agencies.

Five teachers at Central City High School have been involved in teaching experimental and control sections since the beginning of the program. Three of these teachers have received training in the use of curriculum materials and the conduct of course-related activities from staff members of the Constitutional Rights Foundation. In-service workshops have been conducted regularly over the past several years. The workshops have also been attended by the chair of the social science department and the assistant principal in charge of curriculum. During the current year, the CRF staff is offering an intensive three-week workshop with sessions twice a week. The workshops are attended by personnel from Central as well as from other high schools in the area.

Initiation and evolution of the program. The Law and Society course had been approved by the Central City school board in 1974 as an elective for all high schools throughout the city, and for several successive summers the board offered a series of training workshops designed to instruct teachers in appropriate content and teaching strategies. Several Central High teachers attended the workshops, and the course was established at Central in the 1975-76 academic year. Since its inception, there have always been six sections of the course taught each year.

Central faculty members prepared an application for funds from the ESEA Title IV-C program to support the activities of the new course, and although the proposal was prepared in a short period of time, it was approved after only minor revisions. Once funds became available, the sections were divided into the experimental and control groups, and funds were used to support the additional activities of the experimental sections.

A major change occurred in the program during the second year, when a Student Action Group (SAG) was created to assist in program development and to participate in community activities. Most of the students in SAG are drawn from the experimental sections, but membership is open to students in the control section at Central as well as to other students throughout the city. The group receives its primary direction from the project director at Central, with assistance from the nearby CRF staff. SAG recently completed its first major project, publication of a manual listing the local social agencies which provide services for teenagers with law-related problems. The manual covered such topics as birth control, pregnancy, child abuse, drug abuse, income tax assistance, labor laws, legal aid, runaways, suspension from school, rape, criminal victimization, and voting. The students contacted all relevant agencies in the city, gathered information on their services, and produced a 20-page manual which was subsequently distributed to all high-school students in the city.

Many members of SAG intend to keep the group together to work on new projects. One participant describes the group as "our family away from home." The students have a great deal of affection for one another and draw emotional support from their joint activities.

Future of the program. The program is now in its fifth year of operation. If it can be demonstrated in the evaluation that students show evidence of statistically significant differences in legal knowledge when compared to the control group, the program will be accepted for state-wide dissemination. The program director and faculty would like to see the course validated by the state, but they are aware of the need to modify both course and content and activities to meet local needs before it could be used effectively in other urban and rural areas. For example, appropriate new networks of community resource organizations and personnel would have to be developed in each locale.

There is legitimate concern on the part of the program staff as well as the district school office that the program will not be validated because of methodological difficulties in the evaluation. Responsibility for the evaluation was assigned to the city school board, and the evaluation portion of the budget was maintained by the board office. A faculty member from a local university was hired as a consultant to conduct the evaluation, but his efforts and assistance were minimal. Despite repeated efforts on the part of the program staff, the consultant has never yet visited Central High School. He has issued instructions for data-collection activities by telephone, and he did not complete all of the analyses promised or submit a final report.

Should the project be validated by the state board of education, it will continue to be an elective at Central City High School. However, without a continuation of the grant, the experimental and control sections component of the course will be dropped. The additional financial support for out-of-class activities which distinguish the experimental from the control sections will undoubtedly be severely curtailed. Given the methodological problems perceived by the state board of education and the expectation that continuing fiscal constraints will plague the city school system, it appears unlikely that the project will continue to receive additional grant support. This is, of course, a source of great disappointment to both Central's staff and the CRF staff.

Evaluation. With the assistance from the staff of CRF, a number of evauation efforts have been undertaken. A number of data collection activities have been undertaken each year, the most extensive being in 1978-79. All students then participating in the program were given four different instruments as both premeasurements and postmeasurements:

1. a cognitive multiple-choice test to measure student knowledge, comprehension, and understanding of the legal and justice systems;
2. the Defining Issues Test developed by James Rest to measure students' level of moral development;
3. a semantic differential test to measure student attitudes regarding selected aspects of the criminal-justice system;
4. individual interviews with a sample of students in both the experimental and control sections to solicit their views regarding the course, law enforcement agencies, and, more generally, the criminal-justice system.

A classroom observation schedule was also developed by the evalation consultant. A number of process measures were taken during the school year:

1. a data gathering system that provided weekly classroom observations;
2. field-experience/classroom-visit checklists to determine attitudes toward a particular group, agency, or institution within the justice system; and
3. peer-teaching questionnaires to evaluate the peer-teaching experience from the perspective of both the peer teacher and the peer student.

Data were collected from teachers in the program to obtain their views concerning progress within each instructional unit of the curriculum. In addition, a standard instrument was administered to gain their appraisals of each in-service teacher-training session.

All these materials were collected under the supervision of the university consultant. Unfortunately, the data were never fully analyzed. A confidential final report was submitted to the CRF staff but was not circulated among Central City High School faculty or administration. A brief summary provided the following results:

1. Students demonstrated a significant gain in knowledge of criminal-justice agencies and procedures. The most notable gain

occurred during the first semester, with little additional improvement in the second semester. There were no meaningful differences between experimental and control groups.
2. Results on the Defining Issues Tests were similar to those on the knowledge test. All students showed differences in premeasures and postmeasures. There were no significant differences between experimental and control groups.
3. The student attitude assessment, which was not included as a part of the formal evaluation design required by the grant, demonstrated a slight increase in positive attitudes in the experimental group and no differences in premeasures and postmeasures among the control group.

No systematic analyses were made of the observation and interview data, nor of the information collected from teachers. The results of the evaluation are at best inconclusive. Due to the fact that the program has received minimal support in evaluation from the school board and the university consultant, there is a great deal of dissatisfaction among the faculty and administration at Central. Program staff is convinced that the law course and, particularly, the extended activities associated with the experimental group, are doing a great deal to help the students, and the staff is extremely frustrated by its inability to provide quantitative evidence to support this assertion.

Appendix B
ANNOTATED BIBLIOGRAPHY

Alkin, M.C. *Evaluation comment.* Los Angeles, CA: Center for the Study of Evaluation, 1969. Pp. 2-7.

Proposes a model for evaluation research which focuses on decision making including five major components: needs assessment, program planning, implementation of evaluation, progress evaluation, and outcome evaluation.

Alston, W.P. Comments on Kohlberg's "From is to ought." In T. Mischel (Ed.), *Cognitive development and epistemology.* NY: Academic Press, 1971. Pp. 269-284.

Argues that Kohlberg fails to prove his claim that the empirical stages of moral development also represent a progression toward higher levels of morality.

Beck, C., Sullivan, E., Bradley J., McCoy, N., & Paglusio, S. *The reflective approach in values education: The moral education project, year 3.* Toronto: Ontario Institute of Studies in Education, 1976.

Advocates the "reflective approach" in values education, by which students are stimulated to make inquiries with the goals of helping them examine their values for consistency with each other and with the means being used to achieve them and apply their values consciously and accurately.

Beck, C., Sullivan, E., & Taylor, N. Stimulating transition to postconventional morality: The Pickering High School study. *Interchange*, 1972, *3, 4,* 28-37.

Describes an experimental ethics course in a Canadian high school. Topics in ethics were discussed twice a week for four months, and the results were measured by stage changes on the Kohlberg scale. Not until a year after the end of the course did the experimental students show higher stage positions than the control students.

Bennett, W.J., & Delattre, E.J. Moral education in the schools. *The Public Interest*, 1978, 50 (Winter), 81-98.

A severe criticism of both values clarification and cognitive-moral development, using selected examples from their respective instructional materials to argue that they have the effect of covertly persuading students to accept extremely unappealing principles.

Beyer, B.K. Conducting moral discussions in the classroom. In P. Scharf (Ed.), *Readings in moral education*. Minneapolis: Winston, 1978. Pp. 62-75. (Reprinted from *Social Education*, 1976.)

Specific suggestions on how teachers can use moral dilemmas to engage students in a discussion of moral issues within a Kohlbergian framework. Although the goal is to raise students' level of reasoning to a higher stage, fails to discuss the criteria of "good" or "better" reasoning.

Brickell, H.M. Needed: Instruments as good as our eyes. *Journal of Career Education*, 1976, *2, 3,* 56-66.

Proposes "field-based test development" — the preparation of measures of learning (both cognitive and affective) on the basis of classroom observations of what students actually appear to be learning rather than on the basis of formally stated goals. An interesting supplement to conventional procedures, but does not specify how observers can tell what students do "appear" to be learning.

Bronfenbrenner, U. *Two worlds of childhood: U.S. and U.S.S.R.* NY: Russell Sage, 1970.

The first comprehensive discussion of the consequences of differential child rearing patterns in the U.S.S.R. and the U.S.

Broudy, H.S. *Moral/citizenship education: Potentials and limitations.* Philadelphia: Research for Better Schools, 1977. (Occasional Paper No. 3.)

Calls for a program of moral/citizenship education consisting of two "strands": "practice in moral problem-solving" and "knowledge about values." Warns that such a program cannot be expected to bring about great changes in behavior, because too many other factors affect conduct in morally problematic situations.

Butts, R.F. *The revival of civic learning: A rationale for citizenship education in American schools.* [Bloomington, IN]: Phi Delta Kappa Educational Foundation, 1980.

Reviews the development of the concept of "citizenship" from ancient times to the present, and the theory and practice of "civic education" in the U.S. since the Revolution. Describes briefly some of the educational programs pointing toward a recent revival of civic education, and concludes with a personalized statement of the moral principles which should undergird the political system and education for it in a democratic society.

Campbell, D.T., & Stanley, J.C. Experimental and quasi-experimental designs for research on teaching. In N.L. Gage (Ed.), *Handbook of research in teaching.* Chicago: Rand McNally, 1973. Pp. 171-246.

This essay is the classic and still most comprehensive statement on experimental and quasi-experimental designs.

Caro, F.G. Evaluation research: An overview. In F.G. Caro (Ed.), *Readings in evaluation research* (2nd ed.). NY: Russell Sage, 1977. Pp. 3-30.

Offers a comprehensive overview of the field that unifies widely scattered material on evaluation research, history, and methods, including over a dozen case studies of evaluation research projects.

Christenson, R.M. McGuffey's ghost and moral education today. *Phi Delta Kappan,* 1977, 58, 10, 737-742.

A well-reasoned defense of the proposition that the schools should engage in moral education. Presents a list of 20 values which "we can all accept," and urges that they be taught through "a revival of the McGuffey Reader concept."

Conrad, D., and Hedin, D. Citizenship education through participation. In *Education for Responsible Citizenship* (Report of the National Task Force on Citizenship Education). NY: McGraw-Hill, 1977. Pp. 133-155.

Sets forth "a case for youth participation as a central element" of citizenship education; describes what the authors believe to be the conditions for its effectiveness; and gives many examples of ongoing programs, as well as details of various forms of implementation.

Coombs, J.R. Objectives of value analysis. In L.E. Metcalf (Ed.), *Values education: Rationale, strategies, and procedures. 41st Yearbook of the National Council for the Social Studies.* Washington: NCSS, 1971. Pp. 1-28.

A well reasoned defense of the legitimacy and importance of moral education programs in general, with no advocacy of any particular approach.

Cronbach, L.J. (with Shapiro, K.) *Designing educational evaluations.* Stanford: Stanford University, 1978. (Occasional Papers of the Stanford Evaluation Consortium.)

Level-headed advice about the conduct of evaluations from one of the most astute people in the field. The themes are: make many different kinds of observations, be flexible and adaptive, stay close to the data, rely on good sense and systematic observations rather than on statistical apparatus.

Cronbach, L.J., & Associates *Toward reform of program evaluation: Aims, methods, and institutional arrangements.* San Francisco: Jossey-Bass, 1980.

Cronbach and his colleagues propose that the aim of evaluation research should be to increase understanding on the part of all relevant parties as to program effects. The book proposes new and controversial perspectives concerning the purposes, methods, and uses of evaluation.

Downey, M., & Kelly, A.V. *Moral education: Theory and practice.* London: Harper & Row, 1978.

Central theme is that moral education consists in helping pupils learn how to arrive at moral conclusions in a way that is rational but that also takes due account of the role of emotions. Stresses the importance of organizing the school so that it reinforces moral instruction. Reviews several British moral education programs.

Eisner, E.W. *The educational imagination: On the design and evaluation of school programs.* NY: Macmillan, 1979.

Advocates art criticism as a model for educational evaluation, at least as a supplement to conventional approaches. Develops the concept of "educational connoisseurship" — close, knowledgeable, sympathetic but critical observation of instructional efforts.

EPIE Institute, *Secondary School Social Studies: Analyses of 31 Textbook Programs.* NY: EPIE [Educational Products Information Exchange] Institute, 1976. (EPIE Report No. 71.)

Reviewers were asked to apply a method of analyzing the design of instructional materials to 31 sets of materials for secondary-school instruction in the social studies; several questions about the handling of values issues were added to the method for this project. About half the sets dealt with values in one way or another, mostly at the level of "awareness" rather than skills development.

Fenton, E. The implications of Lawrence Kohlberg's research for civic education. In *Education for Responsible Citizenship* (Report of the National Task Force on Citizenship Education). New York: McGraw-Hill, 1977a. Pp. 97-132.

Describes, in clear, nontechnical prose, the main findings of Kohlberg's research in moral development; discusses the implications of these findings for the goals of civic education; and describes the programs then being devised at Harvard and Carnegie-Mellon in which these implications were to be embodied in instructional and just-community programs. The descriptions and discussions take an uncritical stance toward Kohlberg's work, and the developmental work was at an early stage, but the clarity and logic of the progression from research to classroom practice make this still a valuable article.

Fenton, E. *The relationship of citizenship education to values education.* Philadelphia: Research for Better Schools, 1977b.

Posits six goals for citizenship education, and then examines four types of values education programs to determine the extent to which they foster attainment of the goals. Concludes that none of the programs are adequate to the accomplishment of all the goals, and so sets forth criteria for new, "full" programs of citizenship education.

Flowers, J.V. A behavioral psychologist's view of developmental moral education. In P. Scharf (Ed.), *Readings in moral education.* Minneapolis: Winston, 1978. Pp. 264-270.

Some disparate criticisms of Kohlberg's approach in particular.

Fraenkel, J.R. The Kohlberg bandwagon: Some reservations. In P. Scharf (Ed.), *Readings in moral education.* Minneapolis: Winston, 1978. Pp. 251-262.

Criticism of some of the details of the theory and practice of moral-development education of the Kohlberg type.

Gibbs, J.C. Kohlberg's stages of moral judgment: A constructive critique. *Harvard Educational Review,* 1977, 47, 1, 43-61.

Presents the argument that, while the first four stages in Kohlberg's theory of moral development do meet the criteria of being stages in the Piagetian sense, the last two do not: they are too reflective and formal and occur too rarely to be considered "naturally occurring" stages.

Gibbs, J.C. Kohlberg's moral stage theory: A Piagetian revision. *Human Development,* 1979, 22, 2, 89-112.

Says that many of the criticisms of Kohlberg's theory could be averted by limiting the developmental process to the first four stages and positing an "existential" phase thereafter, in which moral reasoning takes place on an abstract level of discourse, with the different forms of reasoning lacking hierarchical order.

Gibbs, J., Kohlberg, L., Colby, A., & Speicher-Dubin, B.   The domain and development of moral judgment: A theory and a method of assessment. In J.R. Meyer (Ed.), *Reflections on values education.* Waterloo, Ontario: Wilfrid Laurier University Press, 1976. Pp. 19-45.

An elementary statement of the Kohlberg approach to moral development and its measurement. Includes a systematic discussion of the coding and scoring of the Moral Judgment Interview and the complete texts of the dilemmas and the accompanying interview probes.

Guba, E.G.   *Toward a methodology of naturalistic inquiry in educational evaluation.* Los Angeles: Center for the Study of Evaluation, UCLA Graduate School of Education, 1978. (Monograph H.8.)

Defines "naturalistic inquiry" as a form of inquiry in which there are relatively few constraints on either the antecedent variables or the possible outputs and attempts to describe and defend it as an alternative to experimental method.

Hall, R.T.   Moral education today: Progress, prospects, and problems of a field come of age. *The Humanist,* 1978, Nov./Dec., 8-13.

Proposes a "taxonomy of moral education objectives" from psychological, philosophical, and sociological perspectives. Points to a "major unresolved dilemma" of moral education — that either it tends to be indoctrination or it tends to promote relativism.

Hall, R.T., & Davis, J.U.   *Moral education in theory and practice.* Buffalo: Prometheus, 1975.

An effort to formulate an approach to moral education which is systematically derived from both philosophical and psychological considerations (and is thus a combination of rationalist and developmental types). Includes illustrative materials for moral instruction that would be consistent with this approach.

Harmin, M. & Simon, S.B.   Values. In H. Kirschenbaum & S.B. Simon (Eds.), *Readings in values clarification.* Minneapolis: Winston, 1973. Pp. 4-16. (Excerpted from D.W. Allen & E. Seifman [Eds.], *The Teacher's Handbook,* 1971.)

Argues that the most effective way of teaching about values is through values clarification, because it rests on the assumption that values are "relative, personal, and educational" and thus seeks "not to identify and transmit the 'right' values, but to help a student clarify his own values..."

Harrison, J.L.   Values clarification: An appraisal. *Journal of Moral Education,* 1976, 6, 10, 22-31.

A vigorous criticism of values clarification on the grounds that it lacks a "sustained theoretical argument," "the discussion of aims and procedures [is] conceptually unsophisticated," the techniques recommended may be inappropriate and are inconsistent with the stated goals, and there is no accumulation of knowledge or "structured progression towards treatment of a moral question in the appropriate breadth and depth."

Hedin, D.P., & Conrad, D. The Evaluation of Experiential Learning Project: Preliminary findings. Paper presented at the annual meeting of the American Educational Research Association, San Francisco, 1979.

Describes a study, still in its beginning stages, of 30 experiential-learning programs at 19 different schools. Discusses the instruments — mostly of the presented-statement type but some constructed-statement, and most of them devised specifically for this study —and presents some initial findings.

Hedin, D., & Schneider, B. Action learning in Minneapolis: A case study. In R.W. Tyler (Ed.), *From youth to constructive adult life: The role of the public school.* Berkeley, CA: McCutchan, 1978. Pp. 149-167.

A brief summary of the theoretical basis of action or experiential learning, and a description of one specific project of that type.

Hersh, R.H., Miller, J.P., & Fielding, G.D. *Models of Moral education: An appraisal.* NY: Longmans, 1980.

Describes six approaches that have been taken to moral education: cognitive moral development, values clarification, action learning, "consideration" (a variety of developmental), and "rationale-building" and "value analysis" (variants of rationalist programs). For each, gives theoretical and historical background, pedagogical techniques, and criticisms or problems (of an a priori rather than empirical sort). Concludes with an attempt to show how all these could be integrated into a single program.

Hill, R.A., & Wallace, J. *Recommendations for research, development, and dissemination for ethical-citizenship education.* Philadelphia: Research for Better Schools, 1977.

Final report of a project to plan a federal role in promoting "ethical-citizenship education." On the basis of consultations, opinion surveys, a review of the literature, and a conference, all under the guidance of an Advisory Group and a Resource Panel, a number of specific recommendations were made (though evaluation was dealt with only vaguely).

Hill, R.A., Wallace, J., Newcombe, E., & Young, J. *Research studies reporting experimental effects in the moral/ethical/values domain: An annotated bibliography*. Philadelphia: Research for Better Schools, 1977.

Gives abstracts of more than 150 research studies dealing with "the training and acquisition of behaviors, skills, or dispositions which can be termed 'moral' in themselves or can contribute to moral/ethical behavior." Since these were experimental studies, the measures used would rarely be applicable to instructional programs.

Hoffman, M.L.   Moral development in adolescence. In press.

A review of the research on processes of moral internalization. Distinguishes three types of such processes, which are construed as components present to varying degrees in each individual's moral orientation, rather than as stages. The processes are associated with family and peers; no reference is made to effects of school experiences.

Hoffman, M.L.   Moral development. In P.H. Mussen (Ed.), *Carmichael's manual of child psychology* (3rd ed). NY: Wiley, 1970. Pp. 261-359.

A review of the research on psychological factors influencing moral development, with overwhelming emphasis on parent-child interaction. Concludes that moral development seems to proceed along four more or less independent "tracks," rather than in holistic and periodically reorganized stages.

Hogan, R., & Dickstein, E.   A measure of moral values. *Journal of Consulting and Clinical Psychology*, 1972, 39, 2, 210-214.

Describes a constructed-statements instrument, in which respondents are asked to write one-line "reactions" to brief statements. Presents results of trials with small numbers of college students. A curious finding was that persons rated as "morally mature" by this instrument apparently preferred an intuitive to a rational approach for the solution of a moral problem.

Joint Committee on Standards for Educational Evaluation.   *Standards for Evaluations of Educational Programs, Projects, and Materials*. NY: McGraw-Hill, 1981.

Guides for judging the utility, feasibility, propriety, and accuracy of evaluations in education. Because it was developed by a committee representing the American Educational Research Association, the American Psychological Association, the National Council for Measurement in Education, and other professional associations, it is the most authoritative set of standards in the field.

Keasy, C.B.   The influence of opinion agreement and quality of supportive reasoning in the evaluation of moral judgments. *Journal of Personality and Social Psychology*, 1974, 30, 4, 477-482.

Describes two experiments designed to test the influence of agreement/disagreement from others at the same stage or another stage on judgments of responses to moral dilemmas. Agreement was found to influence younger persons more than older. Developmental stage seemed to be important only if it was far removed from that of the individual judging, raising a question about the hierarchical nature of the Kohlberg scale.

Kirschenbaum, H. Beyond values clarification. In S.B. Simon & H. Kirschenbaum (Ed.), *Readings in value clarification.* Minneapolis: Winston, 1973. Pp. 92-110.

Questions the adequacy of Raths' original seven criteria for the determination of a value and suggests that it would be more satisfactory to speak of the "processes of valuing" — feeling, thinking, communicating, choosing, and acting. However, it appears that this reformulation is subject to some of the same objections that were made to the criteria.

Kirschenbaum, H. *Advanced values clarification.* Saratoga Springs, NY: National Humanistic Education Center, 1977a.

An effort to elaborate upon and to update the techniques of values clarification, by one of its principal advocates. Includes very brief reviews of research done on the results of values clarification with students and teachers.

Kirschenbaum, H. Values education: 1976 and beyond. In *The school's role as moral authority.* Washington, DC: Association for Supervision and Curriculum Development, 1977b. Pp. 51-69.

Tries to identify goals, skills, and processes among many approaches to moral education. Suggests areas of research and development that would promote improvements in moral education and methods of dissemination to inform educators about currently available materials and methods.

Kirschenbaum, H., Harmin, M., Howe, L., & Simon, S.B. In defense of values clarification. *Phi Delta Kappan,* 1977, 58, 10, 743-756.

Defines values clarification and its expected outcomes, and makes the claims that, contrary to criticisms, it does have a theoretical basis (in the writings of Raths), and research has shown that it does achieve its aims.

Kohlberg, L. From is to ought: How to commit the naturalistic fallacy and get away with it in the study of moral development. In T. Mischel (Ed.), *Cognitive development and epistemology.* NY: Academic Press, 1971. Pp. 151-235.

Kohlberg's major effort to show that the stages of moral development that he found to exist empirically are parallel to a succession of moral views that is also philosophically more adequate at each higher stage, and consequently that the highest stage which he found in his research is also the most acceptable general theory of morality.

Kohlberg, L.   The child as a moral philosopher. In S.B. Simon & H. Kirschenbaum (Eds.), *Readings in values clarification.* Minneapolis: Winston, 1973. Pp. 49-61. (Reprinted from *Psychology Today,* September 1968.)

A non-technical presentation of Kohlberg's ideas about the stages of reasoning, how they are manifested, the invariance of direction and sequence of movement, their cross-cultural validity, and the potentiality for growth by exposing children to one stage beyond where they are.

Kohlberg, L.   The cognitive-developmental approach to moral education. In P. Scharf (Ed.), *Readings in moral education.* Minneapolis: Winston, 1978. Pp. 36-51. (Reprinted from *Phi Delta Kappan,* June 1975.)

Similar to the preceding, but with more elaboration of the implications for the curriculum.

Kohlberg, L.   The meaning and measurement of moral development. Heinz Werner Memorial Lecture, 1, April 1979.

A discussion of the thinking that led to the Moral Judgment Interview and its scoring procedure, and of how the MJI fares when conventional tests of validity and reliability are applied to it. Kohlberg admits to its weaknesses, but argues that nothing better is available for dealing with his research problems.

Kohlberg, L., & Mayer, R. Development as the aim of education. *Harvard Educational Review,* 1972, 42, 4, 449-496.

Makes the claim that, in contrast to the "romantic" and "cultural transmission" ideologies underlying some forms of moral education, Kohlberg's own "progressive" ideology, resting on "the value postulates of ethical liberalism," is able to reconcile philosophy and psychology. Discusses the educational implications of this idealogy.

Kohler, M.C., & Dollar, B.   Youth service work: An antidote to alienation. In R. Tyler (Ed.), *From youth to constructive adult life: The role of the public school.* Berkeley, CA: McCutchan, 1978, Pp. 174-186.

A general description, with many specific examples, of the work of the National Commission on Resources for Youth, "founded expressly to promote opportunities for responsible participation for youth." One of the considerations in the Commission's work is the ethical value of the participation.

Kuhmerker, L., Mentkowski, M., & Erickson, V.L. (Eds.), *Evaluating moral development and evaluating educational programs that have a value dimension.* Schenectady, NY: Character Research Press, 1980.

Papers delivered at a 1979 conference of the Association for Moral Education. (See Lockwood, Mosher, Rest.)

Law in a Free Society. A civic education project of the State Bar of California funded by the National Endowment for the Humanities and the Danforth Foundation. Santa Monica, CA: Law in a Free Society, n.d.

A descriptive brochure of the rationale and programs of the Law in a Free Society project.

Law-Related Education Evaluation Project, LAW-RELATED EDUCATION EVALUATION PROJECT/FINAL REPORT/PHASE II, YEAR 1. Boulder, CO: The Project, 1981.

Reports on an evaluation of six different law-related education projects which used measures of behavioral change among students, classroom observations, and interviews with teachers and others. However, these are described only in vague ways, and the methods of data analysis also are insufficiently explicated.

Lipman, M., Sharp, A., & Oscanyan, F.S. *Philosophy in the classroom.* Upper Montclair, NJ: Institute for the Advancement of Philosophy for Children, Montclair State College, 1977.

The rationale for teaching philosophy — including moral philosophy — to elementary-school children, together with some suggestions for content and methods.

Locke, D. Cognitive stages or developmental phases? A critique of Kohlberg's stage-structural theory of moral reasoning. *Journal of Moral Education,* 1979, 8 (May), 168-181.

While Kohlberg has done essential pioneering work, he has prematurely placed upon his findings too great a theoretical weight. As a result, the six fundamental theses which underlie his stage-structural theory are all defective in one way or another.

Lockwood, A. A critical view of values clarification. In D. Purpel and K. Ryan (Eds.), *Moral education...it comes with the territory.* Berkeley, CA: McCutchan, 1976. Pp. 152-170. (Reprinted from *Teachers College Record,* 1975, 77 [Sept.], 35-50.)

Discusses three problems in values clarification: inadequacies in the "definition and conception of value," ambiguity in the nature of the proposed instruction, and an apparent ethical relativism.

Lockwood, A.L. The effects of values clarification and moral development curricula on school-age subjects: A critical review of recent research. *Review of Educational Research,* 1978, 48, 3, 325-364.

115

Examines 13 studies of values clarification and 12 of moral development in terms of their internal and external validity, experimental design, sample, definition and measurement of dependent variables, nature of treatment, and type of statistical analysis. However, the qualities of the measurement instruments were deliberately excluded from consideration.

Lockwood, A.L.   The original school board position in the evaluation of moral education programs. In L. Kuhmerker, M. Mentkowski, & V.L. Erickson (Eds.), *Evaluating moral development and evaluating educational programs that have a value dimension.* Schenectady, NY: Character Research Press, 1980. Pp. 193-203.

Posits a school board whose members "are rational, accountable, open-minded, and well-intentioned," and do not all hold Ph.D.'s in education and suggests the kinds of evidence such a board would look for in judging the worth of a moral education program (but says nothing about the measures that might be used to provide this evidence).

Lundberg, M.J. *The incomplete adult: Social class constraints on personality development.* Westport, CT: Greenwood Press, 1974.

Presents evidence that differences among stages of moral development, like difference among stages of cognitive and effective development and of personality development generally, are similar to differences among social classes, and explores the historical implications of these similarities.

Mehlinger, H.D.   Moral education in the United States of America. Paper prepared for the UNESCO Meeting of Experts on Educational Institutions and Moral Education in the Light of the Demands of Contemporary Life, Sofia, Bulgaria, April 1978.

Describes changes in social and cultural conditions that have led some people to suggest that the schools should take greater responsibility for moral education. Discusses the issues that surround that shift in responsibility and various approaches that schools might take in assuming it.

Mosher, R.L.   Moral education: Let's open the lens. In L. Kuhmerker, M. Mentkowski, & V.L. Erickson (Eds.), *Evaluating moral development and evaluating educational programs that have a value dimension.* Schenectady, NY: Character Research Press, 1980. Pp. 213-222.

Makes a plea for "mainstreaming" moral education into the curruculum and broadening the criteria of program "success."

Mosher, R.L., & Sprinthall, N.A.   Psychological education: A means to promote personal development during adolescence. *The Counseling Psychologist,* 171, 2, 4, 3-82.

116

Outlines a series of courses "designed to affect personal, ethical, esthetic and philosophical development in adolescents and young adults." Based on developmental theory, these courses would combine formal instruction with active involvement in such activities as counseling others. Describes and illustrates content of several courses in the series and presents initial evaluation results for those that have been tried.

Mosher, R., & Sullivan, P.   A curriculum in moral education for adolescents. In P. Scharf (Ed.), *Readings in moral education*. Minneapolis: Winston, 1978. Pp. 82-97.

Prospectus for a high school course based on Kohlberg's theory. The distinctive elements of the course are that students discuss their own moral dilemmas as well as Kohlberg's and that they are taught how to counsel and teach others concerning moral issues.

Panel on Youth (James S. Coleman, chairman), President's Science Advisory Commission. *Youth: Transition to adulthood.* Chicago: University of Chicago Press, 1974.

A committee report emphasizing the values of reducing the segregation of youth from adults and discussing various ways —especially work-related activities — of accomplishing that goal.

Patton, M.Q. *Utilization-focused evaluation.* Beverly Hills. CA: Sage, 1978.

A plea for the de-emphasis of the experimental method in evaluation, although the suggested alternatives don't seem to be very different from the procedures the author criticizes.

Peters, R.S.   Moral development: A plea for pluralism. In T. Mischel (Ed.), *Cognitive development and epistemology*. NY: Academic Press, 1971. Pp. 237-267.

A critique of Kohlberg (1971). While admitting the importance of Kohlberg's work, Peters argues that the theory has a narrow empirical base; that morality can be a matter of habit and character trait rather than of reasoning only; and that "justice" is not necessarily the exclusive principle of the highest morality and is, furthermore, often an ambiguous criterion of what morality is.

Peters, R.S.   Why doesn't Lawrence Kohlberg do his homework? In D. Purpel & K. Ryan, (Eds.), *Moral education...it comes with the territory.* Berkeley, CA: McCutchan, 1976. Pp. 288-290. (Reprinted from *Phi Delta Kappan,* July 1975.)

Charges that Kohlberg has persistently refused to deal with "very constructive criticisms" — e.g., that there are respectable alternatives to the morality of justice, that action governed by lower-stage moral thought can be very useful, and that evidence about moral growth collected by others is ignored.

Pittel, S.M., & Mendelsohn, G.A. Measurement of moral values: A review and critique. *Psychological Bulletin,* 1966, 66, *1*, 22-35.

A survey of efforts to measure moral values and related concepts from the 1890s to 1966. Most of them were made in the context of personality research rather than of moral education. Moral values seem generally to have been identified with conventional moral standards in a relatively small number of spheres of action.

Plattner, M.F. The welfare state vs. the redistributive state. *The Public Interest,* 1979, 55 (Spring), 28-48.

A provocative criticism of the Rawlsian theory of justice, on grounds of both its internal inconsistency and its implications for "liberal society." Points out that an approach to moral education based on justice as its primary principle cannot claim to be "natural" or unarguable.

Porter, N., & Taylor, N. *How to assess the moral reasoning of students: A teachers' guide to the use of Lawrence Kohlberg's stage-developmental method.* Toronto: Ontario Institute for Studies in Education, 1972.

Describes the method of scoring the Moral Judgment Interview, although this guide would probably not be sufficient to enable one to do the scoring. (It should also be noted that the scoring methods have changed several times since this publication, but more current versions are not widely available.)

Provus, M. *Discrepancy evaluation.* Berkeley, CA: McCutchan, 1971.

Advocates the Discrepancy Model of Evaluation, which focuses upon the difference between standards and performances. Evaluation is viewed as a means of generating data that is a useful aid to decision making to change standards, change performance, or terminate the program.

RAND Corporation. *A million random digits with 100,000 normal deviates.* NY: Free Press, 1955.

The standard reference work for obtaining lists of random digits.

Raths, L.E., Harmin, M., & Simon, S.B. *Values and teaching: Working with values in the classroom.* Columbus, OH: Charles E. Merrill, 1966.

The basic work in values clarification. Defines values and "value indicators," states the objectives of value clarification, describes the major methods, and gives tips for teachers on how to get started and how to deal with problems that might arise.

Rest, J. Developmental psychology as a guide to value education: A review of "Kohlbergian" programs. *Review of Educational Research*, 1974a, 44, 2, 241-259.

Describes several efforts to implement Kohlberg's theory in instructional forms. Suggests that a major problem in those efforts was that developmental theory in psychology was too vague to provide a basis for planning day-to-day activities.

Rest, J.R. *Manual for the Defining Issues Test: An objective test of moral judgment development.* Minneapolis: The author, 1974b.

Detailed instructions for administering and scoring the DIT and guidance in interpreting the scores. Includes a discussion of research on the instrument's reliability and validity.

Rest, J.R. New options in assessing moral judgment and criteria for evaluating validity. Paper presented at the meeting of the Society for Research in Child Development, Denver, April 1975.

Defends the DIT against the criticisms that only interviewing can reveal a subject's moral-development stage; that the DIT " confounds structure with content"; and that it doesn't permit the placement of an individual at a particular stage of moral development.

Rest, J.R. *Development in judging moral issues.* Minneapolis: University of Minnesota Press, 1979.

A thorough review of the usefulness of the Defining Issues Test as an instrument for the measurement of moral development.

Rest, J.R. Basic issues in evaluating moral education programs. In L. Kuhmerker, M. Mentkowski, & V.L. Erickson (Eds.), *Evaluating moral development and evaluating education programs that have a value dimension.* Schenectady, NY: Character Research Press, 1980a. Pp. 1-12.

A call for a new theory of moral education that would combine Durkheim's emphasis on socialization with Piaget's and Kohlberg's on maturation.

Rest, J.R. The Defining Issues Test: A survey of research results. In L. Kuhmerker, M. Mentkowski, & V.L. Erickson (Eds.), *Evaluating moral development and evaluating education programs that have a value dimension.* Schenectady, NY: Character Research Press, 1980b. Pp. 113-120.

A brief description of the DIT and summaries of research results indicating its uses and limitations.

Riecken, H.W., & Boruch, R. *Social experimentation: A method for planning and evaluating social intervention.* NY: Academic Press, 1974.

Written by a committee of the Social Science Research Council, this volume presents a detailed and technical discussion of social experimentation and program evaluation, addressing the advantages, limitations, and practical possibilities of evaluation research as well as a thorough treatment of the major scientific and technical issues of design and measurement.

Riles, W.   The role of the school in moral development. In *Moral development: Proceedings of the 1974 ETS Invitational Conference.* Princeton, NJ: Educational Testing Service, 1975. Pp. 69-79.

Suggests that the most effective way for the schools to play their role in developing common values among all individuals, and in helping individuals to develop their own values, is by offering an exemplar of moral behavior.

Roethlisberger, F.J., & Dickson, W.J.   *Management and the worker.* Cambridge: Harvard University Press, 1961.

This volume is the original and complete report of the famous Western Electric series of studies which produced the now classic concept of the "Hawthorne effect."

Rokeach, M.   *The nature of human values.* NY: Free Press, 1973.

A discussion of the methods and uses of the Rokeach Values Survey, which includes moral principles among many other things.

Rosenthal, R.   *Experimental effects in behavioral research.* NY: Appleton-Century-Croft, 1968.

This volume reports Rosenthal's findings concerning the effect of the experimenter's expectations on subject performance, including the now-famous experiments showing that teachers' "knowledge" of students' I.Q. scores influences subsequent student performance.

Rossi, P.H.   Critical decisions in evaluation studies. In W.B. Schrader (Ed.), *Measurement and educational policy: Proceedings of the 1978 ETS Invitational Conference (New Directions for Testing and Measurement*, No. 1, 1979). San Franciso: Jossey-Bass, 1979. Pp. 79-88.

Argues that evaluations should be done only in certain circumstances, and that when done they should be conducted in such a way that the resulting information is useful to decision makers.

Rossi, P.H., Freeman, H., & Wright, S.   *Evaluation: A systematic approach.* Beverly Hills, CA: Sage, 1979.

A comprehensive treatment of the methods and problems involved in conducting evaluation research in field settings.

Ryan, K., & Thompson, M.G.   Moral education's muddled mandate: Comments on a survey of Phi Delta Kappans. *Phi Delta Kappan,* 1975, *56, 10,* 663-666.

Results of a survey in which Phi Delta Kappa members were asked questions about the meaning of "moral," their preferred institutional influences on the moral thinking and behavior of children, and their attitudes toward possible roles for the school.

Sanders, N.M., & Klafter, M. *The importance and desired characteristics of moral/ethical education in the public schools of the U.S.A.: A systematic analysis of recent documents.* Philadelphia: Research for Better Schools, 1975 (Publication No. BJ-3).

Analysis of the content of educational goal statements collected from state departments of education and private and professional organizations, with primary reference to their concern with moral and ethical topics.

Scharf, P. Evaluating the development of moral education: A response to the critiques of Flowers, Sullivan, and Fraenkel. In P. Scharf (Ed.), *Readings in moral education.* Minneapolis: Winston, 1978a. Pp. 288-297.

Admits that many criticisms of Kohlberg's work are warranted, but concludes that other approaches to moral education suffer even more from defects of empirical truth, educational utility, and philosophical adequacy and consistency.

Scharf, P. *Moral education.* Davis, CA: Responsible Action, 1978b.

A superficial discussion of Kohlberg's theory of moral development and instructions on how to use the theory in various subjects of the curriculum and in the organization of a democratic school community.

School's role as moral authority, The. Washington, DC: Association for Supervision and Curriculum Developmnent, 1977.

Contains essays by R. Freeman Butts, Donald H. Peckenpaugh, and Howard Kirschenbaum on various issues in moral education.

Scriven, M. The methodology of evaluation. In R.W. Tyler, R.M. Gagne, & M. Scriven (Eds.), *Perspectives of curriculum evaluation.* AERA Monograph Series on Curriculum Evaluation, N. I. Chicago: Rand McNally, 1967. Pp. 39-82.

Introduces the now classic distinction between formative and summative evaluation and advocates that evaluators have overlooked the utility of the former.

Scriven, M. Prose and cons about goal-free evaluation. *Evaluation Comment,* 1972, 3, (4), 1-4.

The article in which Scriven first put forth the concept of "goal-free evaluation," as a way of emphasizing that an evaluator should be concerned with the *actual* rather than with the intended effects of a program.

Selltiz, C., Wrightsman, L.S., & Cook, S.W. *Research methods in social relations* (3rd ed.). NY: Holt, Rinehart, and Winston, 1976.

This third edition of the now classic introductory textbook for research methods in the social and behavioral sciences is still one of the best available.

Simon, S.B., & deSherbinin, P. Values clarification: It can start gently and grow deep. *Phi Delta Kappan,* 1975, 56, *10,* 679-683.

An essay in praise of values clarification, with many examples of strategies for using it.

Simon, S.B., and Kirschenbaum, H. (Eds.). *Readings in values clarification.* Minneapolis: Winston, 1973.

A collection of articles, most of them previously published, expressing various viewpoints on approaches to moral education, including those other than values clarification.

Simpson, E.L. Moral development research: A case study of scientific cultural bias. *Human Development,* 1974, 17, *2,* 81-106.

A criticism of Kohlberg's work from an anthropologist's point of view. The main contentions are that Kohlberg presents inadequate evidence for the "universality" of his stages, attributes to development what is more likely to be the product of culturally specific learnings, and greatly underestimates the depth of diversity among and even within cultures.

Stake, R.E. The countenance of educational evaluation. *Teachers College Record,* 1967, 68, 523-540.

Contains the description of Stake's Countenance Model of evaluation research, which concentrates on antecedents, transactions, and outcomes, each of which is examined from four vantage points: intentions, observations, standards, and judgments.

Stewart, J.S. Clarifying values clarification: A critique. *Phi Delta Kappan,* 1975, 56, *10,* 648-688.

Criticizes values clarification for its confused philosophy, inadequate psychology, and faulty methodology, and concludes that "in spite of its significant and positive influence," it has "some potentially serious, even dangerous, problems and implications."

Stufflebeam, D.L., et al. *Educational evaluation and decision making.* Itasca, IL: F.E. Peacock Publishers, Inc., 1971.

Presents the CIPP (context-inputs-process-product) model of evaluation research, which concentrates on four classes of decision making and proposes four related types of evaluation activities.

Suchman, E.A. *Evaluative research.* NY: Russell Sage Foundation, 1967.

This early treatment of evaluation research describes the techniques used to empirically measure the extent to which the goals of social action programs are achieved, to locate the barriers to the achievement of these goals, and to discover the unanticipated consequences of social actions. The book discusses conceptual, methodological, and administrative aspects of evaluation.

Sullivan, E.V. *Moral learning: Some findings, issues and questions.* NY: Paulist Press, 1975.

A history of the Moral Education Project of the Ontario Institute for Studies in Education, and a discussion of a (separate) "practicum" for teachers of moral education. Concludes with reasoned arguments in support of moral education programs, answers to their critics, and practical suggestions for how they can be conducted constructively.

Sullivan, E.V. Kohlberg's structuralism: A critical appraisal. Toronto: Ontario Institute for Studies in Education, 1977.

Contends that Kohlberg's theory of moral development is based on the premises of "liberal" and "western capitalist" thought and therefore cannot claim to be universal; and that Kohlberg's highest stage is impersonal and abstract, neglecting the moral values of personal caring and of community.

Sullivan, E.V., & Beck C. Moral education in a Canadian setting. *Phi Delta Kappan,* 1975, 56, *10,* 697-701.

Describes three experiments in moral education, with comments on how the effects were evaluated.

Sullivan, P.J. Implementing programs in moral education. *Theory into Practice,* 1977, 16, 2, 118-123.

Practical suggestions for factors and people to take account of, and tactics that would be effective, when introducing concepts of moral education into the curriculum. Based on the author's experience in teaching moral education in Tacoma.

Superka, D.P., Ahrens, C., & Hedstrom, J.E. *Values education sourcebook: Conceptual approaches, materials analyses, and an annotated bibliography.* Boulder, CO: Social Science Education Consortium, 1976. (ERIC No. ED 118 465).

Presents a typology of five approaches to values education: inculcation, moral development, analysis, clarification, and action learning. In a chapter on each, explains the approach and describes specific sets of student and teacher materials in prose and in terms of a checklist of characteristics. Concludes with an annotated bibliography, similarly divided, and a more general bibliography.

Wasserman, E.R. Implementing Kohlberg's "Just Community Concept" in an alternative high school. *Social Education*, 1976, 40, 4, 203-207.

Describes the origin, functioning, and perceived outcomes of the first "just community" established within a Kohlbergian program.

Webb, E.J., Campbell, R.T., Schwartz, R.D., & Sechrest, L. *Unobtrusive measures: Nonreactive research in the social sciences.* Chicago: Rand McNally, 1966.

The original source of the concept of "unobtrusive measures." Presents a rationale for their use and discusses and illustrates several types: physical traces, documentary records, and observations both simple and "contrived."

Wehlage, G., & Lockwood, A. Moral relativism and values education. In D. Purpel & K. Ryan (Eds.), *Moral education...it comes with the territory.* Berkeley, CA: McCutchan, 1976. Pp. 330-348.

Urges that a distinction be made between "moral and nonmoral value judgments," because the latter are "legitimately relativistic" while the former are not. Finds that some moral education programs fail to make the distinction and thus apply the relativism of nonmoral judgments to moral judgments as well. Sets forth criteria for "a defensible moral point of view which avoids relativism."

Weiss, C.H. *Evaluation research.* Englewood Cliffs, NJ: Prentice-Hall, 1972.

This short paperback textbook is still one of the best and most popular treatments of evaluation research.

Wilkins, R.A. If the moral reasoning of teachers is deficient, what hope for pupils? *Phi Betta Kappan*, 1980, 62, 8, 548-549.

When the Defining Issues Test was administered to 55 teachers-in-training in Australia, the scores suggested that many of them would be at a lower moral stage than their students.

Wilson, J. *Practical methods of moral education.* London: Heinemann, 1972.

Sets out the "components" of moral education in a special terminology. Shows how these are to be taught, in a rationalist fashion, but also argues that the program must be embedded in a far-reaching restructuring of the school on the model of the family and including "experiential" as well as academic learning.

Zalaznick, E.   The just community school: A student Perspective. *Moral Education Forum*, 1980, 5, 2, 27-32.

An "alumnus" of a Kohlbergian just community tells what it was like. Although it was "an exciting, stimulating, and mutually beneficial experience for students and teachers alike," there were concerns about "moral intimidation, abuse of the stage hierarchy, and the negative effects of the 'halo effect' in moral stage development."

Appendix C

SOURCES OF INFORMATION
AND ASSISTANCE

Carnegie-Mellon Education Center (Carnegie-Mellon University, Pittsburgh, PA 15213)

> Develops programs for advanced training of teachers; conducts
> workshops, research and other activities associated with curriculum
> development; promotes research into educational methods and
> content at the secondary and higher level. Center of development
> for the Civic Education Project, a developmental type of program
> directed by Dr. Edwin Fenton.

Center on Evaluation, Development and Research (Phi Delta Kappa,
Eighth Street and Union Avenue, Box 789, Bloomington, IN 47402)

> Publishes a quarterly and a newsletter aimed particularly at educa-
> tional practitioners, issues monographs and occasional papers,
> and conducts symposia, usually followed by publication of the pro-
> ceedings. Operates under the sponsorship of Phi Delta Kappa, the
> professional fraternity in education.

Center for Moral Education and Development (Graduate School of
Education, Harvard University, Cambridge, MA 02138)

> The research and development center at Harvard University, which
> houses the activities of Lawrence Kohlberg and his colleagues. The
> Center supports a full program of research, instruction, and publica-
> tion activities. In recent years, it has sponsored summer institutes in
> moral development and particularly the techniques of scoring
> moral judgment interviews.

Center for Youth Development and Research (48 McNeal Hall, University of Minnesota, St. Paul, MN 55108)

Does research in evaluation of youth services, curricula for initial training for work with youth, and action learning for high-school students. Publishes an annual report, a quarterly newsletter, and research monographs. Maintains resource collection.

Character (1245 West Westgate Terrace, Chicago, IL 60607)

Describes itself as "a periodical about the public and private policies shaping American youth." Its statement of purpose says that "able academics should increase interdisciplinary efforts directed at identifying causes of and possible solutions to our youth character problems." Each issue usually contains one article; an editorial by the editor, Edward L. Wynne; and several letters to the editor. Published monthly by Character, a nonprofit corporation.

Constitutional Rights Foundation (6310 San Vincente Blvd., Suite 402, Los Angeles, CA 90048)

A private, nonprofit organization which conducts research and produces curriculum materials for law and citizenship education. Curriculum materials are supplemented with a wide variety of activities involving cooperation and interaction with local bar associations, justice agencies, and other government institutions. Regional offices are also located in Chicago and Philadelphia.

Directory of Evaluation Consultants (The Foundation Center, 888 7th Avenue, New York, NY 10019)

Describes background and capabilities, and gives addresses and phone numbers, of more than 650 individuals and organizations that design and conduct evaluations or help others to do so. Includes regional, specialty, and personal-name indexes.

Educational Resources Information Center (ERIC) (Dissemination and Improvement of Practice Program, National Institute of Education, Washington, DC 20208)

An information system designed to facilitate access to the literature on education. In addition to the central office at NIE, it consists of 16 clearinghouses, each specializing in a subject area; a computer storage and retrieval facility; a document reproduction service; and an index-publication service. Computer searches and other assistance, as well as a microfiche collection, are available at each of the clearinghouses. Those likely to be most pertinent to evaluation in moral education are Social Studies/Social Science Education (855 Broadway, Boulder, CO 80302) and Tests, Measurement, and Evaluation (Educational Testing Service, Rosedale Road, Princeton, NJ 08541).

Ethics in Education (PENWISE, Box 1166 Lunenburg, Nova Scotia, Canada BOJ 2CO)

Aims at extending knowledge, acceptance, and especially practice of "ethical/moral/values education" in elementary and secondary schools. Contains articles on historical and cultural perspectives on ethics; case reports of practices and problems in teaching of ethics; news of conferences, developments, and experiments; and "capsule reports on resources." Published monthly September to June.

Journal of Moral Education (NFER Publishing Company, Darville House, 2 Oxford Road East, Windsor, Berks., S14 1DF, England)

Contains scholarly articles and book reviews on theory and practice of moral education. Published three times a year. Available in microform.

Law in a Free Society (515 Douglas Fir Drive, Calabasas, CA 91302)

A project of the Center for Civil Education, a nonprofit corporation affiliated with the State Bar of California. It develops and distributes curriculum materials for K-12, including teacher staff development and classroom multimedia instructional materials covering eight fundamental social and political concepts: authority, privacy, justice, responsibility, participation, diversity, property, and freedom.

Mershon Center (The Ohio State University, 199 West 10th Ave., Columbus, OH 43201)

A research and development center at the Ohio State University concerned with citizen competence, which conducts research and produces curriculum materials. The Center has close ties with the American Political Science Association's committee on precollegiate education.

Moral Education Forum (Hunter College, City University of New York, 221 East 72nd Street, New York, NY 10021)

Quarterly journal of the Association for Moral Education. Contains articles, interviews, bibliographies, descriptions of new research, information about experimental programs with a value dimension, and reviews of relevant books and doctoral dissertations.

National Commission on Resources for Youth (36 West 44th Street, New York, NY 20036)

Publishes a quarterly newsletter and in other ways seeks to foster the principles and practice of community service and action learning.

National Humanistic Education Center (110 Spring Street, Saratoga Springs, NY 12866)

A conference and resource center "devoted to furthering theory, research, and practice in humanistic education." Conducts workshops and provides consultation services, especially for teachers interested in developing a values dimension in their instruction. Issues many publications and maintains a library. Center of development for values clarification.

Northwest Regional Educational Laboratory (710 S.W. Second Avenue, Portland, OR 97204)

Develops products, on its own or in collaboration with others, in areas of instructional systems, career education, and technical assistance. Directs the Research on Evaluation Program, for research, development, testing, and training designed to create new evaluation methodologies for use in education. This project publishes a newsletter which is sent free on request.

Research for Better Schools (444 North Third Street, Philadelphia, PA 19123)

A federally funded organization devoted to improving schools through technical assistance and research and development, especially in areas of basic skills, career preparation, citizenship education, special education, and urban education. Publishes numerous special reports and papers. In 1976-77, conducted a project called Planning for Moral/Citizenship Education, which surveyed activities, sought to crystallize issues and made a set of planning recommendations; a series of reports on this program was published.

Social Science Education Consortium (855 Broadway, Boulder, CO 80302)

Offers workshops in analysis and use of innovative social science curriculum materials and methods; provides information and consultation services; serves as contractor for ERIC Clearinghouse for Social Studies/Social Science Education. Publishes newsletter and other materials and maintains Resource and Demonstration Center.

Social Studies Development Center (Indiana University, 513 North Park Street, Bloomington, IN 47401)

Engages in development of instructional programs in social studies at elementary and secondary levels, research on effects of school climates on students' attitudes, diffusion of innovative ideas and practices in social studies, and promotion of collaboration among individuals and organizations seeking improvements in social studies. Sponsors publications and maintains an extensive library.

The Union College Character Research Project (207 State Street, Schenectady, NY 12305)

A series of longitudinal studies conducted since 1935 has been undertaken by the Character Research Project, originally focusing on Christian education. The research has broadened to include the development of moral and ethical values and the role of the family in human development. The project emphasizes research and development, training and consultation, publication, and dissemination.